This Book is a Gift

from

_____

To

_____

On

_____

"*Even when you'd lost everything you thought there was to lose, somebody came along and gave you something for free.*"
- Jenny Valentine.

"*A book is a gift you can open again and again.*"
- Garrison Keillor.

Your Gift Is Your Power

Helen Uche Ibezim

SEVHAGE
PUBLISHERS
2015

ISBN: 978-978-53799-8-3

SEVHAGE Publishers
S23, Top Floor, No 62, Old Otukpo Road, Makurdi

Administration and Correspondence:
S23, Top Floor, No 62 Old Otukpo Road,
P. O. Box 2192,
Makurdi, Benue State, NIGERIA.
http://sevhage.wordpress.com
http://vershage.wordpress.com
sevhage@gmail.com
Makurdi. Karu. Abuja. Ibadan.
P.O. Box 2192, Makurdi, Benue State
+234 (0) 807 358 0365; +234 (0) 809 248 7423

Book Layout/Design: Servio Gbadamosi for www.winepress.pub
Cover Concept/Design: Su'eddie Vershima Agema and Gabriel Agema

For further information, please contact:
Helen Uche Ibezim
P.O. Box 11049 Garki,
Abuja.
Tel: +2348057268605, +2347083612496
Email: uchelenibezim@yahoo.com

Acclaim for Helen Uche Ibezim's *Your Gift Is Your Power*

Wisdom, which may be translated into the Igbo language, as '*Amamihe*', is not such a common commodity in contemporary Nigerian society. Among other factors, wisdom is what many Nigerians need badly to be able to wade through or meander through a society or community so richly endowed by the Almighty God with human and natural benefits yet so deficient in virtually every index of development. To successfully live in Nigeria or be attached to those who are or seem to be doing so, the average Nigerian needs proper ethical orientation as well as right cognitive style and preferences more now than in time periods before (when and where mutual help and filial disposition ensured that everyone weak, vulnerable and unable was carried along with others who were better endowed). It is within this declining societal scenario that a volume devoted to assisting the less endowed and the ones now disoriented concerning their natural God given talents by the myriads of confusing and conflicting societal situations becomes fit, proper, indicated and relevant. The author has demonstrated that she is a concerned Nigerian of today who knows and believes that no matter the odds (and the odds must always be with us) one can utilise one's God's given gifts, whether intellectual, emotional, spiritual and otherwise to achieve one's cherished goals for the benefit of the wider community. This volume deserves merited study more so that it has been written in readily comprehensible style and reader friendly language. The author is very much herself namely, experienced, witty, confident, hopeful, enthusiastic, enduring, loyal and achieving. She represents a novel class of Nigerian writers who are exploring new and less conventional and still appropriate literary prompts in persuading their readers to achieve the most of their ambition as well as promise. I recommend this volume which I believe is well motived as well as reasonably spiritually inspired.
- Professor (Mazi) O. C. Nwana
Emeritus Professor of Education, Teacher, Humanist, Concerned Traditionalist, and Christian Knight

"Uche Ibezim's *Your Gift Is Your Power* is an inspirational writing that would motivate people to overcome barriers in order to maximise their potentials for effective living. The reality of information contained in this book and the skilfully-blended style make the book appealing to all. I recommend

this book for every school and family."
- **Professor Julie Okpala (rtd),**
University of Nigeria, Nsukka.

Your Gift Is Your Power is an amazing exposure of Helen Uche Ibezim's life, garnished with 26 illustrative poems, and with quotations from Ancient Greece (Socrates) to the present day (Oprah Winfrey). This book is studded with information which can be mined by students at all levels of educational data at which Helen has taught. As I recommend this book for continuous study, I expect students to help extend the limits of this endless source which enlarges with exposure."
- **Professor Anezi N. Okoro**
Acclaimed Author & Professor of Medicine
Author of The Village Headmaster, One Week, One Trouble, The Village School, The Flying Tortoise.

"This book is a masterpiece, and a product of painstaking research on how to build people, and to create a better society. I recommend it for the use of all schools in Nigeria. The book possesses every essential ingredient required for moulding and nurturing the characters of the youth, and indeed all Nigerians. I am yet to experience a more inspired writer than its author."
- **S. G. Okoli,**
Author of 'Legends Of Our Time', & other books.

"Uche Ibezim is a limit breaker, a reality writer, a trail blazer, and a motivational speaker, whose motivation cannot be fully described. She believes that everyone can become the best he or she wants to be, irrespective of one's antecedents. Idea is the wheel that propels the wheel of life, so, Uche, dream on; the world is waiting to hear from you."
- **Adarabioyo Samuel Bigheart,**
Graphic/Web Developer.

"This book written by Helen Uche Ibezim, a gifted and proven 'All-Rounder', spiced with nuggets for easy understanding is indeed an invaluable gift to every reader. A sure spur to awake your endowed potentials to spark off the fire in you. A firewood is an ordinary wood with potential for fire. A wood without contact to fire will eventually rot away. Let the fire in this author fire you up to the springboard to maximally exploit your potentials towards actualising your destiny.... An excerpt from the intellectual wealth of a 'Mother with touch of excellence'. Read on to flourish from her expertise, legacy, and enduring experiences as a seasoned administrator, motivator, and mentor, all expressed in letters."

- Godson Iheanyi Akwada,
Managing Director, Giak Ventures Limited

"It is my singular honour to endorse this book: *Your Gift Is Your Power*. This is a must read for all and sundry. It provides information on how to optimise the use of one's talents. It is an inspirational book for ALL."

-Hajia (Dr) Mrs. Fatima Abdulrahman,
National President, All Nigeria Confederation of Principals of Secondary Schools (ANCOPSS).

~ Dedication ~

To all my students and staff, whose passion for excellence and loyalty gave me the opportunity of being their Mentor. The joy of having produced many leaders of tomorrow shall always live in me, and give me a sense of direction.

Contents

~ Poems That Back Up The Chapters ~

Acknowledgements

To God be all honour, glory, splendour, majesty, and adoration. All strength comes from Him. I sincerely appreciate Him for the knowledge, grace, and wisdom He gave me, to come up with this work. Due to His awesomeness, I was equally energised to compose all the poems that complement every chapter of the book. In fact, the writing of this book has compelled me to confess that "writing a book is NOT writing an ordinary essay." I am very grateful to my divine Leader.

My very special thanks go to my ever warm and caring husband, Obum, who has been my strength, my pillar, my great supporter in all my endeavours. His patience, warmth, encouragement, understanding, and care, during the period of the writing of this book, and even at almost every other time, cannot be measured. He equally took time to edit and make useful suggestions towards the finesse of the production. God will bless his moral and financial contributions towards the perfection of this book.

Worthy of mention is the valuable contribution of my children - Nnamdi, Chike, Nneamaka, Somtochukwu, Chinwe, Emmanuel, and Nmachukwu, my jewels of inestimable value. They furnished me with current information on the entertainment industry, and other contemporary issues, which formed part of my writing. Of special note is little Nma's constant supply of fruits to me whenever I was on the writing desk. That was really motivating.

I am sincerely indebted to the Director of FCT Universal Basic Education Board, Dr (Mrs.) Catherine Ezeilo, who wrote the foreword for this book. Equally, those, whose endorsements have humbled me, are the highly renowned writers and national figures, the pride of this nation, who sincerely demonstrated their appreciation of my work. They include: Professor Anezi Okoro, author of the popular novel *The Village Headmaster*; Professor O. C. Nwana, author of *UNIVERSITY ACADEMICS IN NIGERIA: Memoirs of an Insider*; Mr S. G. Okoli - author of *Nigeria Will Surely Rise Again*; Hajiya (Dr) Mrs Fatima Abdulrahman - The National President of All Nigeria Confederation of Principals of Secondary Schools (ANCOPSS); Samuel Bigheart - Graphic/Web Developer and Mr Iheanyi Akwada - Managing Director, Giak Ventures Ltd. I am grateful to all of them.

I wish to acknowledge, in a special way, Professor (Mrs.) Julie Okpala, Professor of Geographic & Environmental Education, in whose London residence I wrote some of the chapters of this book. She made my stay in the United Kingdom a very pleasurable and memorable one. Professor Okpala was also a super motivator, as she continued encouraging me in my writing throughout the period of my stay with her. Her sincere advice was quite invaluable and led to the enhancement of the quality of this book.

My special gratitude also goes to my in-law, Mazi Kaycee Igwegbe Odum, for his moral and physical support, especially in his immense and sincere assistance to me on some privileged information and contacts, prior to the publication of the book. His mobilisation prowess is really a great gift from God. He is not just an in-law to me, but, a faithful and reliable brother. His wife, Ifeyinwa Igwegbe, my dear sister, was equally of great assistance to me in the course of writing this book. Her sincere concern for my successful outing knew no bounds, as she continuously made useful suggestions towards the final production. Her love, which she shares to all and sundry, especially in her professional calling as a nurse, has always been a source of motivation to me.

I acknowledge the efforts of those who assisted me in the typing of the draft manuscript of the work - Mrs. Okoro, Nonso, and Chika, whose speed on the keyboard led to the early printing of the initial copies of the work. I am also heartily grateful to all those who took time to edit this work, especially, Su'eddie Vershima Agema, a professional editor himself, and his SEVHAGE team, particularly Debbie Iorliam and Aôndosoo Andrew Labe, who undertook the professional editing of the book.

Of immense value is the great impact of my computer instructor, John E. Daniel (PhD), who devotedly taught me how to be independent on the use of computer. The knowledge I got from him enabled me to do some of the typing of the work to my taste. This led me to type all the poems here, by myself, after composing them. I was equally empowered to edit the manuscript of the work, before going for professional editing of the book. Indeed, he spared me the fish and gave me a fishing net in that area of knowledge.

I cannot forget the special motivation given to me by Mr. S. G. Okoli, an author himself, who inspired me to go on with the publication of my book. He displayed his full support and enthusiasm when he freely gave me two of his wonderful books: *Nigeria Will Surely Rise Again* and *The Legends of Our Time*. His advice and sincere contributions were simply overwhelming. I am proud of him and his works.

In another special way, I wish to appreciate the pioneer staff and students of JSS Kurudu, Abuja, and JSS Karshi, Abuja, who all gave me support and love during my tenure as the Principal of the two schools. As a pioneer principal and pioneer staff of the two schools, we all carried the 'load' of establishing virgin schools, but, which have transformed to standard schools today. The experiences I gathered from the two schools, as an administrator, gave me a lot of insight into what the school system should really look like. My findings and the way forward, which will be of much relevance and assistance to the government in power, have been carefully showcased in the pages of this book.

I remain thankful to all those who have touched my life in one way or the other; whose lives bless me; who have faith in my writing, and equally motivated me to go ahead in my project. Finally, I salute all those whose moral backings encouraged me to go for the publication of this book. Thank you all.

Foreword

The world cannot move forward without innovations. Innovations come through ideas from people. This has been demonstrated in the pages of this book, through the author's use of ingenuity, humour, citations, personal, and professional experiences, to reach the readers.

The various topics treated in the chapters of this book are realistic and captivating, as they all deal with contemporary issues which we all need to face squarely. This makes the book invaluable. It is like a wonderland which will take anyone that reads it, on an interesting journey of pleasant discovery of the jewel one possesses. No chapter is less important than the other. Consequently, I urge the readers to pay attention to every chapter, as they are all encapsulated with juicy packages.

The book is unique in many ways: every chapter of the book is blended with a poem originally composed and written by the author herself. This is an indication of how creative and innovative she is. This action, I believe, is to fully capture the attention of the reader, to the reality of the facts she expresses in every chapter. This is quite interesting as students and general users will fully enjoy and appreciate the rhyming nature of all the poems here. Equally, the concrete and humorous citations by the author, of real and daring life experiences, will place readers in a very comfortable mood, to relax and assimilate the facts and the entire contents of the all inspiring work she did in the pages of this book.

I feel this is a book for everyone, because the author has carefully addressed issues that pertain to everyone, irrespective of their areas of affiliation - students, teachers, administrators, parents, public servants, political office holders, girl-child, boy-child, the unemployed, and so on. What I see in this book is a thorough piece of work geared towards making everyone realise his or her worth in the society, so that the nation will be a truly sanitised one, devoid of rancour, corruption, restiveness, and, most importantly, illiteracy. It is a book one has to open again and again in order to answer the question of what one has to offer to himself, the family, and, the society at large. It opens our eyes to the fact that every one of us, from cradle to adulthood, was delicately fashioned and created by God, with unique gifts and abilities which, when explored, make us awesomely beautiful and excellent.

Experience, we often say, is the best teacher. This expression is fully demonstrated by the author, as she takes us down the memory lane of her professional work in the education of the young ones, who are truly the leaders of tomorrow. To learn from a truly experienced teacher and administrator is a thing of joy and satisfaction, because, one is drinking from the correct source of water. This is why I highly recommend this book to all students, teachers, administrators, and even other public servants, as they all have relevant issues tackled in the pages of this inspiring book.

Helen Uche Ibezim has proven through *Your Gift Is Your Power* that she has the prowess of words and expressions to state her concern for the unlocking of potentials, which are caged in individuals, especially, the young ones. I observe that this is a worthy approach to inspiring each one to realise, not only that he/she has a gift, but also, the power of that gift! It will really amaze you to find out that the 'little' gift you possess can bring about huge success for you, and showcase you to the world. The knowledge you acquire from this book will help you to be a positive impact maker. It is left to you to do something positive now, in order to be an asset, not a liability, in your own generation.

The book is commendable, and, is a great and valuable companion. I heartily congratulate the author, Helen Uche Ibezim, for her boldness in expression, thorough research, sincere creativity, and beautiful layout of the book.

Dr (Mrs.) Catherine Ezeilo
Director
FCT Universal Basic Education Board, Abuja.

PREFACE

I am moved by the rate at which many people have died – and are dying - from ignorance. Ignorance is a state of being uninformed, having no understanding, knowledge, education, or awareness. I have been called in spirit several times to write a book. I have only recently obeyed the call – resulting in this. I feel this is a practical demonstration of what you, dear reader, will discover, is preached in this book. Everyone should appreciate the gifts they are endowed with. Once a gift in someone is appreciated and optimally utilised, it becomes a powerful instrument for the person to excel.

Martin Luther King, Jr., the most important voice of the American civil rights movement, stated: "Nothing in all the world is more dangerous than sincere ignorance and conscientious stupidity." Equally, it is interesting to note that James Madison, the 4th President of the United States, and who is famous for writing the first drafts of the US Constitution, which eventually became the Constitution of the United States, categorically said: "Knowledge will forever govern ignorance and a people who mean to be their own governors must arm themselves with the power which knowledge gives." The realisation that one has the capability to identify his talent and unlock his own potential is really empowering. This has motivated me to write this book.

I see myself as one being in a position to get others informed. My experiences as a classroom teacher, a Head of Department in a school system, a Dean of studies in another institution, a Senior Mistress (Academics), a Vice Principal (Administration), a School Principal, an Inspector of Education, and a Co-ordinator of many other established organisations and associations, have given me the impetus to write boldly on my findings and consequently, empower the uninformed on the need to unlock the potentials in them, through the gifts they have.

Experience, it is often said, is the best teacher. I have seen it all in the area of student management, staff management, school management, and general administration. The various workshops I have attended, locally and internationally, also exposed me to some of the findings presented in this book. In this work I have adopted simple diction, to avoid any complications in theme, message or delivery. I know my target audience – students, teachers, parents, unemployed, physically challenged, business men & women, government officials, political office holders, administrators, girl-child, and boy-child. It is not my wish to write for writing sake, but rather, to convey a message.

My days as a classroom teacher and a school administrator were all dedicated to the ultimate grooming of the leaders of tomorrow, most of whom I am proud to note are successful today. Most of them I am honoured to say, humble me with their pride of my being their mentor. With what experience I have, I consider it timely to obey that clarion call, and bring pen and paper together, to make my own contribution towards human development, through intellectual means. As a '*builder*', which many of my associates call me, and '*a woman of vision*', which some groups have tagged me, this is another way of demonstrating societal concerns.

I have thought of a gift to all and settled on this ... It is a present for all time. This, of course, is simply echoing Garrison Keillor, an American author, story teller, humorist, and radio personality, who observed that: "A book is a gift you can open again and again."

Be empowered with this token.

INTRODUCTION

Due to the cogent need for people, both young and old, to identify their talents, and start working on them, to fully attain their potentials in life, many attempts have been made by various writers, poets, and keynote speakers, to tackle the issue. There are a lot of people who have their talents caged and consequently, find it difficult to come out from the cocoon. Others have visibly started using their talents, but not optimally.

This book aims at sensitising people that they have innate abilities in them; special gifts. The gift of each person is his power, if well utilised. Each person is unique and that uniqueness needs to be showcased in one way or the other. Those whose talents are still under lock need to equip themselves with the correct keys of unlocking such. This is to pave way for attaining one's full potential.

It is disturbing to note that many people have not yet realised their worth, thereby relegating themselves to the background. Anne Frank (1929-1945), a German-Jewish teenager, who wrote an amazing diary, from her hiding place during the Holocaust - the mass murder of Jews by the Nazis during the Second World War, sensitised us thus: "Everyone has inside himself a piece of good news! The good news is that you really don't know how great you can be, how much you can love, what you can accomplish, and what your potential is!" Youths are supposed to be challenged by this quote by a mere 16 year old girl!

While x-raying the need for unlocking one's potential, which of course, is one's power, mention is made of some dangerous games people play, and which directly or indirectly affect them in the course of attaining the potentials in them. From every point of view, everyone - child or adult, is involved. The dangerous games are not, however, stated, without proffering ways of escaping from them. The various keys to unlocking one's potential are discussed here too. So, this book is for everyone, as we all have a future to hold dear to our hearts.

My experiences as an educationist and an administrator of schools are equally brought to bear, to help the reader appreciate the practical aspect of the issues raised here. They were not written by a mere observer, but a participant in the process of education. I watch, with deep concern, young talented people wasting away, due to non-commitment to the use of their talents. I strongly see with Ben Herbster, an American protestant clergyman, who was active on social issues such as civil rights, in his saying: "The greatest waste in the world is the difference between what we are and what we could become." Imagine the waste!

Every chapter is supported with a poem, originally composed and written by the author, to offer a little relaxation and fun to the reader, while going through the pages of the book. Each poem depicts the contents of the chapter where it is featured. Poems allow us to look beyond the surface, as a matter of fact. The poems here are very simple, and are a medium through which I have been able to express various notes on chapters in verse. They will, at the same time, move the reader to think deeply (I hope), open him up, and give him exciting moments, while the message is being conveyed.

Chapter 1

You Have A Gift!

A gift is a special ability. It is a quality bestowed by nature. It is also something special that one has and should be grateful for. We should note that gifts are blessings, and blessings are gifts. There exist exceptional gifts like creativity, sports, academics, acting, speech, leadership, debating, drawing, dancing, singing, humour, and so on. They are innate and can be worked upon. There are also spiritual gifts like prophecy, healing, interpretation of dreams and speaking in tongues that we have no control over. Sometimes, you don't have an idea of why you have that special ability or talent but somehow, you just have it. It is God given.

Apart from physical skills, we experience God's gifts, or better still, His blessings, in many other ways: being a father or a mother; having parents or having children or siblings. This is the gift of family that should not be taken for granted. Being in a good position, having freedom, strength, and victory, are also gifts because you never know how special they are until you lose them. In the same way, love is a gift from God which is what He is; God is love. Love gives you joy and an unexplained feeling, which makes you happy.

Everyone has a gift for something, even if it is the gift of being a good friend, according to Marian Anderson, one of the best American contraltos (women with lower singing voices) of all time. A friend is a gift from God, because God gave you this precious person to remind you that you are not alone. This can be classified under the gift of friendship. Your gift makes room for you and brings you before great men. Therefore, you need to acknowledge the gifts you have.

The worst crime anyone will commit is to think he is cheated by nature. If you feel you are cheated by nature, try to look around you and find out the number of people who are endowed with what you have. Of great note is the statement by Helen Keller, an American prolific author, political activist, and lecturer, who was the first deaf and blind person to earn a Bachelor of Arts degree, "I cried because I had no shoes until I met a man who had no feet." If you are relegating yourself to the background, you need to be motivated by this emotional speech which is really encouraging. William Arthur Ward, a motivational speaker, author, and one of America's most quoted writers of inspirational maxims, posed a relevant question, thus: "God gave you a gift of 86,400 seconds today. Have you used one to say 'thank you'?"

This is food for thought, and should cause you to be grateful.

Abundance of Gifts

The various gifts that exist set people apart from one another. Gifts have been shared to everyone in a way that no one will have monopoly of all the gifts. A particular gift may be favourable to one person, while another type of gift will be favourable to another. A person may have a lot of money, but she may not have children who will partake in the wealth. Another person may be poor and wretched, but with an uncontrollable number of children. Another one may have wealth and children, but may be lacking good health. Looking at all these prevalent situations will make us feel thankful for the various gifts we have. Voltaire, one of the greatest French writers and philosophers, famous for his wit, equally admonishes us that God gave us the gift of life, it is up to us to give ourselves the gift of living well.

However, human beings are insatiable and selfish. This is why people keep dying of envy and jealousy. Thank God for your abilities and blessings, rather than complain of another person's own. There is this practical example: a certain woman, gorgeously dressed, was riding a jeep and passed by a woman who was shabbily dressed and begging in the street with her triplets. The gorgeous woman murmured: "God, look at this woman, blessed with triplets, when I don't have even one. Oh! This world is cruel to me." Equally, the shabby woman cried out: "God, look at my fellow woman, driving such a big car, and I am dying of hunger here, with my kids!" This builds a picture of our forgotten blessings, and our insatiable wants. The truth is that none of them is cheated and we cannot always have it all. Each one of them has her own gift to cherish; only that they decided to ignore this and concentrate on what they don't have.

Every Day Is A Gift From God

You have the special gift of producing something tangible for both yourself and others as long as you are alive each day. It is up to you to hold on to the gift of each day. Joel Osteen, a famous American preacher, in his book, *Every Day Is A Friday,* says we have to realise that every day is a gift from God which we need to celebrate. Why waste the gift by gnashing your teeth, grumbling about vanities in life, thinking about things that do not really bring positive changes in your life?

When you decide to shun all the negative aspects of life around you, you will automatically be swimming in the gift of joy and happiness. Instances abound where certain poor or sick people, despite their wretchedness and what may seem to be a hopeless condition, never allow such to weigh them down. Rather, they start thinking of what benefits they have derived from life. That is the reason why Joel Osteen admonishes us thus: "Faith is always in the present. Your attitude should be: I'm excited to be alive at this moment. I'm excited to be breathing today. I'm excited about my family, my health, and my opportunities. I have plenty of reasons to be happy right now... You may have some setbacks and your circumstances may change, but don't let that change your mind... Keep it set on happiness. It is your choice to be happy. Make up your mind to enjoy this day, to have a blessed, prosperous and victorious year." If we recount all the gifts we are bestowed with, we shall always think positively and act positively. Accept each day in your life as a gift from God.

Show Gratitude

Gratitude is a powerful life virtue. When you are not grateful for what you have, even that may be taken away from you. The mouths of some people are filled with only complaints. Remember the popular saying that "If you complain, you remain, but if you praise, you'll be raised." When your mind starts grumbling, the best approach is to pick a pen and paper and start writing down the things that are working right for you. Other people around you may not even have such endowments, they may not have such opportunities, but you do. Is it not a special gift? Think about your health: you can see, you can walk, you can make use of your hands and legs, you can hear, and so on. Which begs the question: Are gifts only material possession? No. You need only to think of how you would be without certain attributes like your sight for you to get an idea of this.

Have you ever pondered that a healthy person is said to be a wealthy person? If you are in doubt, pay a visit to patients of various degrees of sickness. Get an idea of how much they spend on drugs alone. Even if you are sick, what about people who have passed on, through such sickness? Complaints will not change your situation; rather, they will pull you down. Restrain from such practice, and be grateful. Being grateful can change your life. Reminding yourself to be grateful is one of the best things you can do for yourself. Being grateful will earn you a lot of goodies in such a way that you will live longer, you will be more popular, you will be in a better mood, you will be more resilient, you will be more generous, and you will attract more realisation of your wishes.

Gratitude helps you realise what you have and this naturally lessens your need for wanting more all the time. When you are grateful, your health improves, and this reduces stress. This practice helps you see the good in every situation so that you will be in the right mood not to complain and stay stuck.

Your Gifts Should Not Be Taken For Granted

We fail to realise the true value of many things in our lives until they get missing. It is like the popular saying: you don't miss the water until it runs dry. For instance, a person may be blessed with hardworking and caring parents. Such a person might spend all the time gallivanting about town and 'enjoying' life not adhering to his/her parental instructions. The day such a person loses them, the person will hate the person's self and consequently, live a life of regret. Equally, some parents may have a promising young child, but they will never think of taking proper care of the child, in terms of his daily needs, and probably, educational requirements. When death or any other ugly incident takes away that child is when they will realise they have lost a precious jewel.

There is a popular saying that "You don't know the value of what you have until you lose it." Some people take their gifts for granted, and do not ever like to use them to make positive impacts. The unfortunate thing is that such people do not realise this until the opportunity has come and gone.

You may be endowed with the special gift of empowering people with your wealth, but you decide to be selfish and wicked. What happens when you lose it? You were probably thinking that wealth was meant for you alone. There is a reason for every gift. Ask yourself why you are privileged to be blessed in any special way. The answer will enable you never to take your gift for granted. Use it wisely for it to be fruitful and beneficial to others. But what if you decide to be selfish and wicked? What happens if you lose your wealth? Who do you turn to?

In relationships, some people take their spouses for granted. A person may be very hardworking, trustworthy, responsible, and caring, but may unfortunately be taken for granted by his or her partner. Endurance may prevail for a while but the person taken for granted may also get tired of enduring.

Always appreciate what you have, and never relegate it to the background. Appreciating the gift of having someone who cares for you and makes your life comfortable will do you real good. Do not ever take things for granted, because they might not be there tomorrow.

Dump The Quantity And Uphold The Quality

It is not really how much, but how well, that matters. Whatever you find worth doing should be done well. In essence, whatever you do should not be done for the simple sake of doing it, but for the worth of doing it. The story is told of an old man, aged 112 years, who went to consult a medical doctor, and the following conversation ensued:

> *Doctor*: Papa, what can I do for you?
>
> *The old man*: Doctor, my problem is that I can no longer see clearly.
>
> *Doctor*: (Laughs) Papa, at the age of 112 years! What have you not yet seen?

This sounds funny, but the fact remains that the old man still desired quality life.

I do not believe in ordinary numbers, but the content. I would rather buy an expensive drug which will give me lasting satisfaction, than a cheap one which will give me lasting misery. The irony is that the joy of buying a cheap drug disappears immediately and imposes a long-lasting bitterness on the patient. On the other hand, the bitterness of buying an expensive drug does not last long, as this is easily replaced with the joy of regaining your health.

A quality life, using your gift, matters a lot. Bring out the best in you, to enjoy life's great potentials. Taking what is just good for you will improve your life quality. It is not the number of years you live that matters, but the positive achievements you have been able to record. Don't be quick to say: "Do you know how long I have worked here?" You may be there, but the place is still empty! Think instead of the input you have made.

Are You At Your Best?

You can become 'unstoppable' if you decide to do the work you wish to accomplish. Tupac Shakur, an American rapper, songwriter, and actor, one of the best-selling music artists of all time, once said: "I want to grow. I want to be better. You grow. We all grow. We're made to grow. You either evolve or you disappear!" Your personal growth is dependent on how eager you are to be at your best. You may be presently blessed with a certain skill, but you can still learn new skills and habits.

In the school system, for instance, after exams, the teachers are expected to make entries of the results of the students inside the report booklets. Such teachers, counsellors, form teachers, and head teachers, are expected to make comments regarding the students' performances in the class. The comments that are common include: "You can still do better"; "Work harder next time"; "Do not relent in your efforts"; "There is room for improvement," and so on. All these are geared towards motivating someone to be at his/her best. You can always do better.

Dance To The Tune

Are you obeying your calling or neglecting it? It is interesting to see a dancer performing well, but awful to notice another dancing out of sync with the music. This is equally the same with our gifts. Some people foolishly follow others to do what they are doing, without knowing that they have their own specific type of music they are called to dance to. We need to know that it is one's gift that paves way for one. As is stated in the Bible, "A man's gift maketh room for him, and bringeth him before great men" (Proverbs 18:16). If you are called to play football, for example, and you reject it, to move over to acting, the likelihood of succeeding is minimal. On the other hand, if you are gifted in acting, and you want to turn to 'Mikel Obi' overnight, just because you have heard of the number of honours or trophies he has won, what is the guarantee that you can make it?

Dr. Steve Maraboli, a life-changing speaker, bestselling author, and Behavioural Science Academic, in his book, *Unapologetically You: Reflections on Life and the Human Experience* says: "You have a unique gift to offer this world. Be true to yourself, be kind to yourself, read and learn about everything that interests you, and keep away from people who bring you down. When you treat yourself kindly and respect the uniqueness of those around you, you will be giving this world an amazing gift... You!" What an inspirational quote!

Every song has a dancing step. You can avoid missing the steps when you know the style. Nobody will expect me, for instance, to go and start singing, because I will surely disappoint that person since I cannot sing well. But I will gladly accept to write the wordings to the song or even dance to that!

Talking of dancing, dancing to someone else's tune might send you to uncomfortable bondage if you do so blindly. You have your own muscle, your own motion style, so why not dance to your own tune and bring out that hidden gift in you?

Your Gifts Influence Others

One important thing about your gift is that it encourages others. When people around you witness how you are positively using your gifts, they will be pushed to open their hearts to find out their own gifts. By this practice, the society is filled with gifted people, who are really reaching others positively, enriching them. As a matter of fact, God gave us gifts to benefit others. Likewise, other people's gifts are for our benefits.

A musician's influence for example, is that the people around him are made happy. Music is used to entertain people. Music can equally be used for relaxation of the body and soul. A person endowed with the gift of cooking well naturally endears people to herself. People will eat and enjoy the meal to nourish their bodies. The gift of a great farmer is such that people around him can never die of hunger. Food, we all know, is a necessity of life.

One who can easily express himself or herself in writing is a worthy gift to the nation. That is why we shall continue to hail great writers like Wole Soyinka, Chinua Achebe, Mabel Segun, Anezi Okoro, Buchi Emecheta, O. C. Nwana, Zaynab Alkali, Maria Ajima, Chimamanda Ngozi Adichie, Teresa Oyibo Ameh, to mention but a few.

The gift of inspirational speech makes an occasion very lively. It is not everyone that is gifted in talking. Someone who is talented in speech can make the audience go bananas, because of the excitement he will inject into them. So, how is your gift influencing others? Negatively or positively? Allow your gift to touch someone today, and influence people positively.

~ Opportunity In Ability ~

1. Making good use of your ability
   Gives you room for great opportunity
   If you apply your own integrity
   You will not wallow in inferiority.

2. You will be empowered to access
   The very true road to success
   But if you decide to digress
   You're not going to progress.

3. If you make your time precious
   And then decide to be serious
   Your life will become so gorgeous
   That people will become jealous.

4. It takes only your courage
   To release what is in storage
   You have yourself to encourage
   To strive for the juicy package.

5. Life is worth being celebrated
   And people need to be decorated
   But people should really be devoted
   For them to be fully elevated.

Chapter 2
Identify Your Talent

A talent is any natural or special gift, special aptitude or ability, which a person is endowed with. Most talents are innate. We came into the world with nothing materialistic but we all came with talents. Your talent is your gift from God. No other person gave you that gift and nobody can take it away from you. The talent you have is not like the other common gifts, such as money, houses, cars, and jewels, which can be regarded as ordinary possessions. Talents come in various forms, and extend into many areas of life. They may be artistic or technical, mental or physical, personal or social. It is a tree that brings forth fruits, if well-watered and nursed. This explains the fact that we need to identify such talents in our lives because they hold the keys to our fortune, fame, joy and of course, future.

Identifying your talent is one major function of a person, in order to forge ahead to be great or successful in life. A tree can never walk up to a man; rather, it is the man who walks to the tree. You do not have to wait for talents to appear. If you never try something, you will never know it. For example, if you do not get involved in singing, you will never know if you can sing or not. You are not going to find a talent without trying anything. A person who has not touched a guitar or piano, can never dream of being talented in guitar playing or piano – or know if he has an innate ability to be good at such instruments. So, in discovering your talent, there is the need to attempt new experiences

Sometimes, there are interests that come naturally to you. You may even do those things without thinking. Check yourself thoroughly, and find out what you do with ease which others struggle to do. You may be in the school or in the office, and have an inclination to certain activities, for example: public speaking, athletics, swimming, football, and so on. Look to your obsession and interests, for the possibility of talent. There is no need wasting your time wishing you had a talent for acting, when you know that you spend all day drawing and painting. Focus on those interests that come to you, and develop them, so that the potential in you will be fully unlocked. Talent is like a muscle. You will lose it if you do not use it, but you have to build it if you want to use it.

If you use your talents wisely, God will give you more. If you use your influence wisely, God will increase your influence. It remains a source of joy that will constantly supply every individual the goodness and greatness of life. It is a precious gift that can be used by a person to excel in life.

It is important to note that when we improve on things we are gifted in, we have the chances of reaching our optimum while we can only reach a stagnated point if we try to do something that we are not naturally gifted in.

Make A Move

No man is without talent. Go online or find a book where you can take a personality quiz to figure out what your temperament is and then perhaps, what you might have a natural ability for. When you learn more about your natural ideas, behaviours, and attitudes, you will be able to figure out more about your talents. Record keeping about your successes, both little and big, will help you identify things for which you might have a talent. When you have a deeper thought about the little successes, you might connect to more significant talents and abilities. Just build on them. You may have, for instance, done a wonderful job planning and organising an event, celebrate that as a success. That may be a strong indication of leadership and managerial skills that will still prove useful in future.

Pay attention to the observations of people around you. If you are unable to pinpoint what you do without a hitch, some other people around you may even be the ones to ring it like a bell in your ears that "You're really good in sports," "You're great at dancing," and so on. That sends a signal to you about your talents, so that you can work on that, to make exploits. Your greatest move should be to uphold the three 'C's in life: Take a 'Chance' to make a 'Choice' to bring a 'Change' in your life.

Make Use Of Your Talents

Your talent is meaningless unless you use it. Maya Angelou, the late famous American author, poet, playwright, director, stage and screen performer, said "I believe talent is like electricity. We don't understand electricity. We use it." Many personalities are being reckoned with, today, because of their ability to identify their various talents, and make optimal use of them. In Nigeria, for instance, many stars today are great users of their talents. In the area of music, for example, there are popular musicians like: Korede Bello (of the famous hit, 'Godwin'), Davido, Tiwa Savage, Flavour, Timaya, P-square, 2face Idibia, Frank Edwards, Don Jazzy, Wizkid, D'Banj, Patoranking, and so on. These musicians have recorded success because of the use of their talents.

Of great interest is the talent displayed by Professor Laz Ekwueme, a Nigerian musicologist. Professor Ekwueme (born 1936) is a man of many parts. Not only is he a master music composer and producer, he is equally an actor, a scholar, a prolific writer, a singer, a choir conductor, a teacher, and a traditional ruler of high esteem. In fact, he is the first Nigerian professor of music. As a man of diverse interests, he is a professor of speech and drama, a professor of Theatre history, a professor of acting, and also, a professor of music. He believes that continuing in one's profession to the end of one's life should be encouraged. He has imparted positively on the Nigerian nation through his various roles, such as: forming the Laz Ekwueme National Chorale (a highly respected African Choral group); organised the University of Nigeria Choral Society; co-ordinated the Nigerian National Choir at the Black Arts Festival, 'Festac '77'; his Chorale was the choir for the Opening and Closing ceremonies of the 8th All Africa Games, COJA (Abuja 2003); the Laz Music Chorale also featured at the Opening Ceremony of the Commonwealth Heads of Government Meeting (CHOGM) in Abuja, December 2003; actively involved in the Nigerian entertainment industry, and so on. He is judiciously making use of his talents, and this practice is worth emulating.

In the area of comedy in Nigeria, we have comedians like: Basket mouth, Ali Baba, Julius Agwu, Akpororo, Omo Baba, I go Die, I Go Save, Helen Paul, Klint Da Drunk, A.Y., Bovi, Gordons, and so on. They are forces to reckon with. People invite them to make their functions exciting, and they are heavily paid for that. While others are having fun, they are displaying and enjoying their talents, and equally, making fortunes out of such.

The area of video entertainment is equally worth citing. It is now much fun for people to relax in their homes, after the hustle and bustle of the streets, and the tight schedules in the offices, to enjoy themselves, with popular home videos. One of such is Nollywood - Nigeria's movie cinema, and the third largest producer of home movies in the world. One fully appreciates the use of talent of acting/drama by these actors and actresses, most of whom are now multi-millionaires. Their power of entertainment makes their pastures to be greener. The likes of Patience Ozokwor, Genevieve Nnaji, Ini Edo, Olu Jacobs, Nkem Owoh, Pete Edochie, Kenneth Okonkwo, Mercy Johnson Okojie, among others, are attracting people's attention on the screen. They are telling their success stories now, due to the use of their talents.

Making use of your talent involves constant practice. Someone who practises, whether it is sports or art, or any other field, will always end up more talented than someone who never does. You cannot expect an artist to be wonderful when he never picks up a paint brush to paint. You need to make your talent real, by challenging yourself to be a master. It needs to be turned into something special. Commit to learning everything about your field, and respecting the complexity of your talent. Do not neglect your talent. You have to commit to building it into a skill. Having a natural talent for playing tennis, for instance, does not mean anything if you do not commit to building it into a skill. Your talent is like a seed that you are planting. Your seed needs to be watered, and weeded, to ensure your seed grows into a big plant. As iron sharpens iron, so does a talented person sharpen another person too. Be close to other talented people, so that you will easily practise routines and attitudes about their talents.

Your Talent Gives You Power

Our great footballers are cherished and honoured because they are using their talents to make the nation proud, and equally, elevating the social status of their various families. It is a thing of privilege for some people to even pose for a photograph with great footballers like Mikel Obi, Victor Moses, Vincent Enyeama, Sunday Mba, Joseph Yobo, Osaze Odemwinge, Kenneth Omeruo, Ogenyi Onazi, Emmanuel Emenike, Ahmed Musa, Kanu Nwankwo[1], and so on. The issue here is that, once you are a star, you are always a star! I cannot forget how elated I was when I posed for a photograph with JayJay Okocha[2], a great Nigerian ex-footballer, in South Africa, some years back, when I travelled to Johannesburg for Pan-African Women Conference. I am still mindful of that picture.

Apart from these Nigerian footballers, there are other ones from other countries, who are recognised worldwide too. These are stars from their various countries: Cristiano Ronaldo (from Portugal), Lionel Messi (from Argentina), Eden Hazard (from Belgium), Arjen Robben (from Netherlands), Neymar (from Brazil), Zlatan Ibrahimovic (from Sweden), Gareth Bale (from Wales), Diego Costa (from Spain), Mesut Ozil (from Germany), Thiago Silva (from Brazil), Karim Benzema (from France), Alexis Sanchez (from Chile), Luis Suarez (from Uruguay), Iker Casillas (from Spain), Toni Kroos (from Germany), and so on. These are people who identified their talent in football, and greatly made, and still make use of this talent. Of course, that is their power now. There are still many of such talents in our young pupils, students, and others roaming the streets. You can still make it in life, identifying with a particular football club, and assiduously playing the game by the rules. Do not be easily put off. It is a negative way of trying to achieve success.

Some people are talented in writing, and this is their power. Today, no one can discuss Nigerian writers without mentioning people like Chinua Achebe,

Wole Soyinka, Ben Okri, Anezi Okoro, Buchi Emecheta, and Chimamanda Ngozi Adichie. Chinua Achebe (1930-2013) is regarded as 'the father of African literature'. His work reveals cultural norms, changing of societal values, and the individual's struggle to find a place in his environment. He is best known for his novel *Things Fall Apart*. Professor Wole Soyinka (born 1934), a playwright, poet, and writer, was the first black African to receive the Nobel Prize Award. His writings often focus on oppression and exploitation of the weak by the strong; none are spared in his critique. One of his great quotes is: "The greatest threat to freedom is the absence of criticism." Ben Okri is equally one of the greatest writers of our time. Born in 1959, author of *The Famished Road,* Ben is a renowned novelist, and poet who was knighted by Queen Elizabeth II for his services to society through the arts especially literature.

Professor Anezi Okoro (born 1929), is one of the Nigerian writers I admire so much, because of the way he engages his readers, through simplicity of words, and humour. Going through some of his popular novels like *The Village Headmaster; One Week, One Trouble; The Village School,* one will appreciate the author's choice of vocabulary in communicating to the reading populace. His books are memorable for being rendered in such graphic language. He uses his ingenuity to hook the reader's attention. Anytime I pick any of his novels to read, I am set to have fun. As a matter of fact, he is a man of diverse talents. Not only is he a renowned author and writer, Anezi Okoro is equally a professor of Medicine, a Consultant Dermatologist, and a Researcher on albinism. Truly, he is one of the great Nigerians who are using their talents to touch various areas of human interest - health, academics, and entertainment.

Buchi Emecheta (born 1944), whose novels draw heavily from her own life, addresses gender imbalance and enslavement, and how women are often defined through the narrow framework of sexuality or the ability to bear children, is the author of *The Joys of Motherhood*. Chimamanda Ngozi Adichie (born 1977), is part of a new generation of Nigerian authors growing in reputation, as her novels have attracted universal acclaim and awards. She is really talented in writing. She wrote the popular multiple award winning book, *Half of a Yellow Sun*, which was turned into a beautiful Hollywood movie.[3]

Also, worthy of note in the display of talents are the works of O. C. Nwana, now an emeritus professor of education. Born on April 16, 1934, Professor Nwana is an accomplished educationist and author of many books, among which are *University Academics in Nigeria: Memoirs of an Insider* and *Introduction to Educational Research*. More than 20 different titles of his are currently on sale in the market. Through his works, many teachers have been empowered with cherished skills in the job of teaching. They have equally been equipped with great passion for the teaching profession. Truly, he is a teacher of teachers. Suffice it to say that anyone who trains teachers is indirectly teaching the entire nation, and most importantly, building the nation, as education is the bedrock of any nation. The history of education in Nigeria can never be complete without mentioning his name, because, he has contributed much in the education sector. Equally, he has empowered people with the knowledge of the history and culture of some towns (for example: Arondizuogu), through his writings. Others are enabled to read and appreciate their town history and social norms, through his talent in writing.

Some people have been empowered through their gifts of running commentary. When we were growing up, there was one little boy in our neighbourhood who was talented in football commentary. He would just stand in front of a big crowd and start making imaginary commentary on football, using the real names of footballers. It was much fun watching him running commentary on a football match. The boy was just about ten years old then. The other children could not do that. They were all busy, admiring him and clapping for him, as he entertained all. Through that practice, the boy was offered scholarship by a philanthropist, up to university level. Today, he is a well-groomed journalist and, in fact, one of the best and most popular national news reporters on the radio in Nigeria. It gives listeners much delight to hear his silvery voice: "This is Chibuike Madu, reporting from Enugu."

What about you? Ensure that you, too, empower yourself with your talent.

The list of human endeavours where people need to showcase their talents is numerous, but the examples mentioned here are just to concretise the point that we all need to identify our individual talents and use them, to progress in life, and make positive impact on others.

Assess Your Life History

When you assess your life history, you will be able to find out the talents within you. Just start thinking of areas where you have been excelling in life. What are the things that come naturally to you, without struggle? Not only will you find out the talent you are using, but you will equally find out the ones that need to be developed.

The bundle of unique abilities, gifts, and talents God has given you is what makes you who you are and sets you apart from others. These talents give you power to impart upon others. As a matter of fact, whether you are an organiser, a cook, a teacher, or an events manager, you were given those abilities to serve others and, equally, empower yourself. Apart from personally finding out your talent, other people around can assist you in knowing your strengths. When you make these discoveries, then you have to create time for new things, in order to expand beyond what you are now. Always assure yourself that your talent is yours and no one else's. The more you know about yourself and how to apply that knowledge to the actions you take, the more happiness and success you experience.

Your Icing On The Cake

It is amazing that some people find a particular task tedious or uninteresting, while you are crazy about it. The fact that you have pinpointed something good, and are using it to excel, is quite rewarding. That's your icing on the cake! Your greatness, through your talents, will start attracting awards, medals, higher recommendations, juicy invitations, and so on.

One of the biggest names in the world of sports is the Jamaican sprinter, Usain Bolt (born August 21, 1986). He is a world-famous track and field athlete. He is a very gifted sprinter, and he utilises the gift optimally. His ability to run very fast has empowered him and given him an edge. He is known for his speed. He became famous as the world's fastest man in 2008. Sports enthusiasts hail him because of his exceptional performances on the track. That is his talent turned into his power.

Equally worthy of note is the American professional tennis player Serena Williams (born September 26, 1981). She is ranked No. 1 in Women's Singles tennis. She is recognised by several sports writers, commentators, and former players as the greatest female tennis player of all time. She recognised her talent in tennis playing and used it to excel. That is her power today. She is now a world-revered figure and has been considered by many, as the greatest woman to have ever played the game. Her performances in the tennis court are quite entertaining, impressive, and exceptional. She holds that as her power and that is the reason for her fame. Her sister, Venus Williams is also a force to reckon with in the world of tennis. Both of them train each day and have never stopped practising.

Since you have the special ability that allows you to do something well, you will be disposed to use that in many rewarding ways. The most successful people in the world are the ones who have found ways to take advantage of their natural talents in the course of their daily activities. They recognise and claim their natural talents, use them in their personal and business lives, and value the talent differences between themselves and others. Success in life is a process that starts from the inside. Building your talents into skills and abilities, in a creative manner, will let you make more exploits in life. Identify your talents today. When you find it, harness it and keep getting better.

~ Make It Real ~

1. Merely looking without reacting
   Will never bring you success
   Moving into full acting
   Is a great experience to access.

2. How sweet you'll find the lofty skills
   As you try to make your own choice
   The joy that follows the thrills
   Will give you a great voice.

3. Taking your time to understand
   What it means to entertain
   Makes the body and soul to withstand
   Every form of negative terrain.

4. It takes just to create a chance
   To allow the muscle to bubble
   And as you get engaged in the dance
   You free yourself from all trouble.

5. Endeavour to make your talent real
   And try to bring out your name
   Thus providing your daily meal
   As you strongly walk into fame.

Chapter 3
Unlocking Your Potential

We all have far more potential power and ability than we are currently using. However, some people do not realise that they have this powerful potential and consequently, do not bother themselves about such. When you look inwards, you will see that there is something you need to do with yourself, to reach that enviable height designed for you. What are your thoughts about yourself? What expectations do you have of yourself? What do you want to attract in your personal and professional life? What do you want to be known for? These are some of the questions that will help you feel the need to unlock your potential and the need for you to be more than what you are presently.

Definitely, you require the ability to have high expectations of yourself (dreams), expectations that you would succeed at what might appear to be a lofty vision. However, you need to be encouraged by the words of Charles M. Schwab, a famous American steel magnate and businessman, known for his manipulative skills and risk taking habit. Schwab once said that none of us is born with a stop-value on his powers or with a set limit to his capacities. There is no limit possible to the expansion of each one of us. Realising that you are going somewhere greater than your present status is a great move into unlocking that potential in you.

Those Childhood Days

I remember how our childhood experiences moved some of us into working towards realising the stuff we are all made of. Amongst the children, you could visualise future actors/actresses, musicians, footballers, teachers, doctors, engineers, lawyers, comedians, and so on. Some of the children were found engulfed in acting some professional roles through drama or plays. Today, some of them are full-time professional actors and actresses. Some others were fond of singing and creating music (playing instruments). Today, too, most of them have become successful artistes. This is because those who were dedicated took their time to work on their abilities which have made them successful today.

Sadly, in those days, comedians were not given full recognition, so, some wasted their talents in comedy by not using that to grow. As a matter of fact, they were regarded as semi-fools. But, good enough, some of them realised they could use it to attain their full potential. So, what is the story today? They are the ones taking the stage, as no one feels that an occasion is complete without a comedian. They are offering health solutions to people who are fully stressed up, and this brings succour and relief to such people, as they are moved to smile, laugh, relax their bodies, and even being relieved of high blood pressure.

Still, on comedy, a comedian once shared this story at a function: "A man came back from church one day and was unusually high in spirit. He went straight to the wife and lifted her up. The wife, who incidentally did not go to church with him that day, felt the husband wanted to rekindle his love for her. So, out of excitement, she asked: 'Honey, what has come over you to lift me up like this?' The husband without missing a heartbeat answered her promptly: 'Our Pastor told us that when we go home, we should lift our problem to God. You're my problem'."

Sure, every normal person would laugh at jokes. This is a therapy that is good for everyone. The comedians found out that the ability to make others laugh and forget their problems would be their selling points, and they developed that ability in a way to making a living from that! So, from childhood, one can work towards the future. This calls for commitment to the call one has.

Take Some Actions

If you are really interested in unlocking your full potentials, you need to take some actions, to pave way for that. Find out your strengths and weaknesses. You should know where you come in strong and where you need assistance, so that you will be able to stabilise your personal life and nurture your professional interactions. Ask yourself the reason for your existence. Definitely, God created you for a purpose. Find out if that purpose has been achieved. Have confidence in yourself and believe in the power of 'Yes, I can'. If you do not trust your ability, how can you move on?

Self-knowledge is very powerful. Identify more strengths that make your weaknesses irrelevant. You may be sociable, reliable, humorous, honest, or hardworking. You may have the technical know-how, computer skills, and acceptable personal traits. Working on the areas where you use to excel will put you on the right track. Ask yourself the things that make you happy and fulfilled. These may include: writing books, teaching other people, sporting activities, and the like. These activities will psychologically move you into acting on what your future has in store for you. Be the hero of your own story. Ensure that you are the one controlling your decisions. These decisions may be on your eating, drinking habit, leisure times, use of time, and your thoughts. You are the one who knows what is best for you, and what you can do. Only make sure that these decisions lead you to living a better life.

Open yourself to different possibilities. There are no absolutes, only options. Empty your mind and think on those possibilities, to know which one you can start embarking on. Identify one thing, small or large, that you really want to accomplish. Decide on a first step, and then do it, no matter what. You may decide to write a book, establish a restaurant, run a school, start a bakery, or so. Whatever your goal is, do whatever you can to get it, then, do everything in your power to keep from losing it. Never underestimate your ability to be a positive influence on someone else. You can be the hero of someone's story. Your special talent will fish you out from the crowd, you know.

Aspire to grow. Do not remain the same. To ensure this, you have to surround yourself with friends and people that are better than you in areas that you want to improve on. You will learn from them. We are happy when we are growing. Always move with the spirit of determination. It is worthy to note what Winston Churchill, a legendary orator, a prolific writer, an earnest artist, and a long-term British Statesman, who twice served as the Prime Minister of the United Kingdom (from 1940 to 1945, and again from 1951 to 1955)[4], said: "Continuous effort, not strength or intelligence, is the key to unlocking our potential."

Be positive. Your positive attitude to life will make you scale through. Naturally, life is full of challenges, but, when you exhibit positive attitude, you will earn success and happiness. It brings optimism into your life. Positive attitude brings constructive changes into your life, and makes you happier, brighter, and more successful. If you are easily distracted, have a rethink and remain focused. Once you are goal-oriented, you will find out that you will be moving with a sense of direction. Discipline yourself to know when it is time to work and when it is time to play. Outline what needs to be done, so that you will be properly guided. Distance yourself from those things that get you easily distracted. Always keep your vision and goals in mind.

Peer pressure can make a child in the school system to make a negative decision concerning his lifestyle. In some cases, the victim is being controlled by the peer group. It becomes difficult for him to take responsibility for his action. Children are advised to be firm with the positive steps they have taken, to make their future bright. Do not be at the mercy of the people who influence you negatively. Once you take the decision not to smoke, for example, do not be convinced to try another stick of cigarette. If you have decided to use your time wisely for studies, do not bow to any pressure group inviting you for one trivial activity or the other. Your choice or decision is something you would have to live with for the rest of your life and as such you do not want to regret your actions in the future.

Do not hold onto the past, but take the experience as a lesson. Use the past experiences to improve your life for the future. This is the simple truth. Just move ahead and make the future better. One of the ways to move ahead is being grateful which will assist you to a large extent. This practice will make you never to feel demoralised. When you show gratitude for the things that make you laugh or smile, you will be more zealous. When you realise that a lot of people out there have it worse off than you do, your spirit will be high.

You'll Be Adored

When you unlock the potential in you, you will be adored. There was a small boy schooling in one of the government schools in Onitsha. He could not do simple calculation, but, dancing was his own talent. The boy lived in the shanty side of Onitsha town with the poor parents who were petty traders. Today, he is a multi-millionaire as a result of the developed potential in him. He is being adored by his mates for his wonderful acrobatic displays which others — the mathematicians — cannot do. For the child who is endowed with the ability of calculation, he followed that course diligently, and eventually, became one of the movers and shakers of our economy today.

All the Nigerian footballers we adore today, for example, Obafemi Martins, Mikel Obi, Osaze Odemwingie, Shola Ameobi, Victor Moses, Emmanuel Emenike, Ahmed Musa, Joseph Yobo, Victor Moses, Sunday Mba, Vincent Enyeama, to mention but a few, reached the peak of this profession, because they did not allow their talents to be caged. When you ask some people the question: "What is your hobby?" Some of them will reply: "Listening to music." Wow! Music by whom? - By another person created by the same God who created them. This is how some great musicians are taking care of other people's *passe-temps favoris* (other people's hobbies) – They satisfy people who take delight in listening to music. These musicians were able to detect and unlock the potentials in them, and they are today being celebrated and adored.

Your Body Parts Play Great Role

All the parts of your body have various roles to play. Check them, one by one, and find out where your prowess lies. Some have made it through the use of ordinary mouth. One popular man in Abuja, Ahmed Isah who has chosen to call himself 'Ordinary Ahmed Isah', and who has the title of 'Ordinary President' of the 'ordinary people', said that his power lies in his mouth. Through a popular radio programme, *Brekete family*, anchored by him, he uses the mouth as his weapon to fight injustice, corruption, and other social ills in the country.

He is a man I admire so much, because of his courage and selfless service. He has been found by many to be using his God-given talent in speech, to bring succour to the less privileged, give a voice to the voiceless, and motivate government officials to sit up in their jobs. What I see in him is in this quote by Brenda Francis, an Irish poet, story writer, novelist, and playwright: "If you have a talent, use it in every way possible. Don't hoard it. Don't dole it out like a miser. Spend it lavishly like a millionaire intent on going broke." The irony is that such people never get broke because they have already made it, and can only progress, rather than regress. Other parts of your body - your hands, your legs, your fingers, your teeth, your face, and so on, can move you into action. Locate the one that will perform the magic, and you are good to go.

Who Will Benefit?

You may begin to ask: who should be the beneficiary of the keys to unlocking one's potential? Funny puzzle, anyway. Everybody is a beneficiary. Everyone needs these keys because everyone has a future to protect and cherish. Children, parents, pupils, students, teachers, administrators, business men and women, the unemployed, physically challenged, girl-child, boy-child, Chief Executives, — all need the strategy to make the best use of what God has given them. When one's potential is unlocked, the significant positive change is glaring. Therefore, unlocking of one's potential is a *sine qua non,* for success in life.

One pertinent question you need to ask yourself is: "Am I, in any way, unique?" Then the next question is: "Is my potential caged?" You will go further to ask: "How do I open it?" If you are able to get to the point of realising what you can comfortably do, without much persuasion or stress, you are on course. That thing that interests you and makes you feel real good can take you to your *El Dorado*. In effect, everyone has the need for unlocking potentials. Come out from the cage and be free with the use of your natural gift.

~ I Earnestly Need It ~

1. In a bid to be a hero
I have to flee from zero
Gathering all the necessary might
To board life's required flight.

2. With all the available capacity
And my enabling audacity
I am equipped with the power
To reach the enviable tower.

3. It is in my expectations
That I make my affirmations
To have a pleasant life
Devoid of any strife.

4. Seeking a way to succeed
Demands hard work indeed
To unlock the potential
Requires the credential.

5. Certain things I have sought
From my innermost thought
And came out from the pressure
To get the treasured leisure.

Chapter 4
The Dangerous Game

The practice of any action that will lead us to our doom is a dangerous game. Many of such practices exist, and, unfortunately, people are often 'trapped' by such unpleasant circumstances. The consequence is that we lose focus on attaining that enviable height we are supposed to reach, to empower ourselves, and the chances of unlocking one's potential will be blocked. Such games are practised everywhere — in the school system, in the church/mosque, in offices, in the markets, and, even in the streets. These games are practices like use of drugs, cheating, lying, stealing, truancy, and so much more. People should not be involved in such practices, as they hinder their ability to fully unlock the potentials in them, through great use of their natural endowments.

Students' Involvement

In the school set-up, students have tricks which deprive them of achieving their goals. Such tricks range from truancy, pilfering, lateness, bullying, absenteeism from lessons, cheating in exams, non-participation in sporting activities, non-involvement in club activities, falsehood, cultism, to drug addiction. All these vices, when curbed, will pave way for these children to obtain far better results, which will enable them unlock their potentials.

The use of hard drugs is one of the world's most contemporary vices. Hard drugs inflame the mind, sedate the heart, and make the body feel 'high.' Hard drug leaves its victim a wretch on one hand and a danger to others, on the other hand. It is these hard drugs that students in higher institutions or even secondary schools take, which make them act in violent ways. This is because meaningful things appear meaningless, after smoking the rubbish. Hard drugs destroy these young ones and make some of them to be mentally deranged later. Their behaviours within that particular period of taking the drugs are completely unacceptable, and it is an unfortunate situation.

Another vice is examination malpractice, which is very common amongst students who are desperate to excel, without corresponding input of labour and diligence. How can you reap where you did not sow? This calls for serious concern, to avoid producing fake graduates and half-baked graduates, who cannot defend their certificates.

The exposure to pornography is eating deep into the emotional life of students. This practice as a vice is becoming rampant in schools. Students are often caught with pornographic videos and pictures which are downloaded into their mobile phones — which, of course, are not supposed to be allowed in schools. Most parents are not aware of this. However, let it be stated fully that this practice kills the psyche of these tender hearts.

A survey of students who have passed out from their various institutions shows that students who really obeyed the school rules and regulations, and who were serious with their studies, are the ones that the society is using today. Many are now professionals in their various fields of endeavour. We have doctors, lawyers, teachers, engineers, architects, and so on. What about the others who were 'small gods' when they were students? Most of them ended up gnashing their teeth due to societal unacceptability. What is the implication of this experience for those who are still in the school? – This is your chance, either to make it or to get lost. The choice is yours.

Teaching Or Cheating The Students?

Teachers play a significant role in the lives of students. Consequently, any negative act by a teacher, through commission or omission, affects the future and subsequent unlocking of potentials in those students. Students are like sheep; therefore, they need shepherds who will conscientiously guide them, for them to be able to attain their full potentiality. The work of a teacher is to teach the students and never to cheat them. As a teacher, your influence affects the life of every student who is in your class. A good teacher is expected to be resourceful, patient, resilient, adaptable, dedicated, creative, passionate, caring, inspirational, empathetic, accountable, determined, compassionate, and, of course, organised. Cheating students, rather than teaching them, is a provocative practice, because, the measure you use to give to others will be the one that will be used to measure for you.

A good teacher loves to teach. Such a teacher will definitely have love and passion for teaching the children under his care. This attitude has everlasting effect on the students. Believe this - these children dread teachers who do not have passion for the profession. Anyone who went through the school process surely and quickly remembers the favourite teachers and the terrific ones. They know teachers who are effective and those who do not change their academic lives positively. An effective teacher is resourceful. He is always willing to think outside the box. He will always be thinking of how to be creative and adaptable to the students' situations, for them to be able to grasp and understand the lesson. A good understanding of the content of what to be taught is what makes a good teacher. The teacher understands the content and knows how to impart that knowledge to the students, for them to understand. As a matter of fact, he plans his lesson very well before going to handle the students. He can never go to the class, unprepared.

A great teacher is the one who is dedicated to his calling. He always comes early to school. He never misses his lessons. He spends extra time, providing students with the best education. Sometimes, he uses part of his weekend to coach the students, especially when they are preparing for examinations. There is no doubt that a good teacher is caring and compassionate. He cares about the success of the children and will do everything positively possible for the students to come out in flying colours, never through cheating, anyway. He figures out the personalities and interests of each student. A real teacher motivates the students through challenges like class activities, assessments, quiz and/or giving them homework. Equally, he does a follow up, in terms of correcting. This is to ensure that students fully comprehend the lesson; he is not involved in a 'make-belief teaching.'

It is unfortunate, to find out that some teachers play on the intelligence of these young ones, by refusing to do the work they have been sent to do. These erring teachers indulge in cheating the students in various ways, such as: missing their lessons; leaving the notes to be copied by the students without their supervision; sleeping in the class, while the students are left to continue with their noise-making; and dressing in provocative ways, thereby distracting the students' attention. This crop of teachers who are cheating the students lack content of knowledge of their lessons before going to meet the students. Instead of teaching, they are cheating the students! How can a teacher go to the class, unprepared, and expect the students to be happy with him or her? There was this funny story of a teacher who went to the class and started sleeping. Unfortunately for him, the inspectors came in and met him sleeping. Thinking that he would play 'cleverness' when he saw the inspectors, he quickly stood up and pretended that he was doing a demonstrative type of teaching, and asked the students: "Class, what am I doing?" They all shouted: "You are sleeping, sir." The inspectors were not impressed! That led to the teacher's dismissal.

A bad teacher is always prone to cheating. Since he finds it difficult and unimportant to fully engage the students during normal lessons, he resorts to aiding and abetting exam malpractice. He freely gives out answers to students in the exam hall, so that they will pass his subject, especially in external examinations. Not only that, he arbitrarily awards marks to students in a test that never took place. You can imagine the damages he is causing to the brains of these children who are supposed to have their brains nourished with the correct stuff, in ways they can easily defend their answers. A teacher who is a cheat is associated with 'I don't care' attitude. He is not mindful of the outcome of the academic endeavours of his students. He is rather sarcastic, and easily disgraces them. Teachers, who are cheats, do not motivate their students through challenges of giving them homework and creativity practices. When they do try to give homework at all, these works will never be marked. I wonder how they want the students to know which answers are correct and which ones are not.

A promiscuous teacher can equally be regarded as a cheat. When a teacher goes into an amorous relationship with a student that is entrusted in his care, he is seriously cheating the student, the school administration, the parents, and the society in general. He fails to realise that the future of the child is in his hands. Of course, there is no way you can keep yam and goat together, because, definitely, the goat will go and eat up the yam. That type of person is not supposed to be in the teaching profession.

Classroom management is a big problem to an ineffective teacher. He cannot control the class effectively, as the students are seen making noise and even eating, while lessons are going on.

An irresponsible teacher lacks professionalism. This is because he is unable to uphold the etiquettes of the profession. How can a teacher be chewing gum in the classroom? How can a teacher dress in such a provocative manner to distract the attention of the students? How can he routinely be absent or late? When the classroom is in disarray, any one standing in front of the class at that time can never be said to be a good teacher. A good teacher always has control of the class and is always engaging the students, to maintain their attention.

However, there are teachers who are diligent and purposeful in their calling. Those who have displayed these positive attributes are enjoying the fruits of their labour, because they have been blessed with happy family lives, good health conditions, and higher appointments. They are the great builders. Their students, on graduation, bless them. The graduates equally reciprocate the teachers' kind gestures with worthy gifts when they are in influential positions. They are ever cherished.

For teachers who choose to be bad, they play a dangerous game with the future of students, our nation and future leaders who would be the ones to either look after them or bury them when their time comes.

Ready For Only Inspectors?

The administrators in the school system are regarded as models for the students under their leadership. Any bad trait from them affects the students' abilities to unlock the potentiality in them. Naturally, there are good and bad administrators. So, they are not exempted from this dangerous game people play.

A reliable administrator sees to the progress of the growing ones. He is always organised and prepared, knowing *fully* well that things can crop up anytime. He is always conscious of the fact that the future of these young ones lies in his hand, so, he always sits up. An administrator, who cannot comfortably answer questions about the school he is running, is not really answering to his call in a productive way.

Some administrators are only prepared when they hear that inspectors are visiting their schools. As a mark of routine, they come to school only when it pleases them, at the detriment of the children under their care. These are the heads who should be showing good examples to their staff and students. If the main source of water supply is soiled or dirty, where will people go to fetch water? Who do the children look unto, for moral assistance, social disposition, and academic excellence? It is the administrator. Unfortunately, some are very deceitful. They pretend that things are going on well in the school, when, in actual fact, many things are going wrong. It is very sad to find out that some administrators connive with external supervisors, to assist their students in writing external exams. They provide money, materials, and other juicy offers to make these supervisors succumb to their criminal tendencies. This game they play is dangerous and can backfire anytime, any day…

I had a personal experience when I went to conduct WASC examination supervision in one secondary school outside Abuja. That was when I was a Vice Principal in charge of Administration. I walked into the school with the exam papers. All the teachers, including the principal, welcomed me. They gave me the impression that the students were 'ready' for the exam. I was not deceived, though, knowing the inclinations of some cheats in the system. All of a sudden, I started hearing whispers in the exam hall — the whispers of invigilators — the teachers from the school — revealing the answers to the students. I was furious. I shouted at them to stop the condemnable act. I had to call the attention of the school principal, thinking that he was disciplined enough to address the situation. To my greatest dismay, he, too, was part of the act! I pursued all of them from the hall. *What a hell!*

So, those deceitful administrators are never in a position to identify the children's talents easily, worse still they do not care. However, conscientious administrators, of course, see themselves climbing higher. Worthy of note are some school administrators who are now higher government officials. Some have served as ministers and some are still serving as ministers, ambassadors, high commissioners, and so on.

Inadequate Provision Of Infrastructure

A dangerous game played by the government is in the area of inadequate provision of infrastructure for schools. These basic infrastructures are the tools required for the unlocking of potentials in the children who are in those institutions. Some schools lack library facilities, ICT centres, potable water, access roads, science equipment, and so on. These are hindrances to attaining a successful academic programme.

Some schools lack teachers in specific subject areas. The areas some students are excelling lack the appropriate teachers to handle such subjects. How do you expect a student who has the potential of becoming a medical doctor to attain that height when he is not provided with teachers in relevant subjects such as Physics, Chemistry, and Biology? At the junior secondary school level, without a Basic Science teacher to handle the foundation level, how will the student cope when he enters the Senior Secondary School? Of course, it is not possible to fetch water with basket. A basin or bucket is needed. This is true.

The teachers need to be given the full incentives, to enable them discharge their duties. Without proper motivation, nothing meaningful can come up. Knowing fully well that teachers are the bedrock of the nation, calls for higher incentives for them. After all, if there are no teachers, there would be no President, Governors, Administrators, Politicians, and so on. Every success in the history of any nation is attributed to the teachers' efforts in educating the populace. This issue of training and retraining of teachers can never be regarded as waste, because the teachers are the ones holding the nation's economy, through the products we expect from them. Government should always give them a cause to smile.

The Parents' Responsibility

Some parents have left the training of their children entirely in the hands of the teachers. We should not forget that the home is the first school/institution of the child. There is a popular saying I used to share with my students: "Some children come from homes; some come from houses; while others come from jungles." Which one is applicable to your family?

A conducive environment in the home is the therapy for a child's positive growth. If a child does not have a sense of direction, he will never know what he wants in life. Remember that, if you do not know your destination point, you can never end your journey. It is wrong to entirely leave the training of your child in the hands of teachers. You need to create time for your children and be close to them. This affords you the opportunity of knowing their strengths and weaknesses, to be able to assist them in coping with the evolving social, psychological and physical problems they may encounter. This is very important in the life of your children.

Lack of proper upbringing can affect the youths when they grow up. When a child is properly trained, he will find it difficult to deviate, when he grows up, unlike the ones who have already been immorally brought up. This is reminiscent of the biblical injunction: train up a child in the way that he should go and when he grows, he will not depart from it. So, parents need to do a lot of homework in this regard.

Social Media - Constructive Or Destructive?

Social media refers to the means of interactions among people, in which they create and share ideas, exchange comments among themselves, in virtual communities and networks particularly the internet. Social networking has become a major part of society today. Many people wake up each day and check social media websites, like Twitter and Facebook, first thing in the morning, instead of reaching for a newspaper, after their morning devotion – for those who even do devotion still. It has become popular for millions of users around the world to exchange information.

The essence of social media is a welcome development. Regardless of distance, through this means, we have the ability to maintain ties with our loved ones, reconnect with friends whom we have lost contact with; work with others,; make new friends; share our day to day life with loved ones; stay informed about the world; share updates, photos, videos, events, messages with our dear ones in real time during the course of any day, and so on. For those in business, they get attention from potential customers; advertise their goods through cheaper means; and equally, work with others, regardless of distance.

Unfortunately, abuse has come in, and is eating deep into the advantages of such services. This causes distraction and time wastage, because of the frequency in using the media. For instance, checking the Twitter feeds by a student rather than studying for exams, is a serious matter. Trying to reply to comments on Facebook in order to please the friends there equally wastes time that would have been used in doing more important tasks. One thing leads to another in the world of social media, and soon precious time is lost browsing, chatting, talking/sharing information, viewing pictures, and the like.

Some people hack other peoples' accounts and start posting things that the original account owner would have no idea about. Others log in with fake profiles, in order to post wrong information and/or probably commit character assassinations. Some log in there to only post obscene pictures, thereby exposing the genuine users to pornography. Many negative things are done there.

But on the same internet, people do research on developing themselves. They learn, update things and do so much more. So, it is up to the users of the media to make a constructive use of such. Opting for the productive aspect of the social media will enable one obtain the information for the necessary growth one desires.

Curbing The Vices

The government should be blamed for some of these negative behaviours exhibited by the youths. When government cannot provide the basic necessities of life, like potable water, electricity supply, good roads, accessible education, child-friendly learning environment, and so on, how will the youths be happy? The government, at every level, is expected to play its key role so that most of these vices will be drastically reduced. Lack of good governance is one of the factors that cause youth restiveness. We should always strive for quality governance in every administrative circle. It can be in the school, offices, state level, or federal level. We ought to remember that the youths who demonstrate usually do so against the injustices meted out to them by those in positions of power.

Good governance makes the youths develop confidence in their leaders. It helps when a government can provide for its citizens in aspects of amenities, job/wealth creation and political direction. Good governance will also stop the youths from demonstrating, after all, what would there be to demonstrate against? The good things being done? The saying that "a poor man is an angry man" is really often demonstrated. Poverty is simply one of the causes of youth restiveness. This calls for the government concern on seeing how poverty can be eradicated. If parents are able to provide what their children need, most of them will not be involved in political thuggery, armed robbery, prostitution, and so on.

Any government that is concerned about the welfare of her citizens is not distracted by side talks; rather, more developmental strategies are embraced, to satisfy the needs of the society; kudos to such governors, legislators, and chief executives. A survey in some states of the federation practically demonstrates where some state governments are fully committed to the development of the states. It is fun to testify here that I am always proud to travel down to my state because of the good network of roads there, the security of the lives and property, and the provision of some basic infrastructure, for the citizens.

Equally to be mentioned is the case of some state governments who are offering scholarships to the citizens, and even paying bursary awards to the ones in higher institutions. Such gestures need to be emulated, rather than being criticised. These are great ways of discouraging the children and the youths from vices. These actions will compel the citizens not to revolt against the government in power, seeing truly that their welfares are being taken into consideration. We should encourage such gestures, in order not to demoralise the good intentions of such governors.

Any society, whether big or small, that allows a good percentage of its youths to be misdirected, risks its future. The positive and meaningful developments across cultural settings are usually engineered, fostered and shaped by the generation of youths in that society. This is because the youths are the greatest assets that any community or state can be proud of. As a matter of fact, they are the greatest investments for society's sustainable development. Unfortunately, youth restiveness and social vices are on the increase, and, consequently, becoming a threat to the concerted efforts to win the battle. Due to the fact that this phenomenon of restiveness leads to breakdown of law and order, economic misfortune, and other resultant consequences, it is always better to prevent, than to cure. The causes of this unacceptable behaviour should be traced and tackled.

Non-recognition of the youths can move them to initiate negative actions, for them to be recognised. It is therefore necessary for these youths to be involved at every level, for their voices to be heard. They should be legally engaged, because, the idle mind is the devil's workshop. In the school system, for example, the introduction of School Based Management Committee (SBMC) is an avenue for the representatives of the students in the school (together with some philanthropists and education-friendly individuals) to be involved in the decision takings and makings in the school. If students are involved in decision making, the incidences of rioting amongst students will be drastically reduced.

In the area of exam malpractice, reading culture should be imbibed by the students. Useful books, magazines, and newspapers should be provided. The more you read, the more knowledgeable you will become. Retraining of teachers should be a regular practice, to avoid obsolete knowledge and ideas. Students should be constantly coached and groomed. Both parents and teachers should live up to their integrity. A well laid foundation leads the child to success.

In effect, this dangerous game, practised by almost everyone, can be seriously curbed. We need to check where we are not getting it right, and carefully dot our 'i's and cross our 't's. An ideal society can surely be achieved, if each person does what is expected of him or her. These vices can be effectively curbed when the government, the parents, the teachers, the administrators, the students, and the entire society perform their statutory roles.

~ You Got It Wrong! ~

1. A game not worth the candle
Is not worth to handle
You cannot just but rattle
In what you regard as battle.

2. A leading way to jail
Has signs that you will fail
You better set sail
For life's ventures that wouldn't ail...

3. If you wish to be royal
You really need to be loyal
Your approach should be cordial and formal
For things to be quite normal.

4. Making a choice for lust
Will take you to the dust
If you don't opt for rust
Neat game will be a must.

5. You have no one to blame
If one can't see your name
But parting ways with shame
Will take you to your fame.

Chapter 5

A Positive Impact

This is a situation of making your mark in an environment in a positive way. Making a positive impact is one of the best ways to find a sense of purpose, sense of belonging, happiness, and fulfilment. Your blessings — material or in kind — can change the lives of others. When you do what you do best, you are helping not only yourself, but the world, too. When you are the only happy person in the midst of several others who are suffering then, there is problem for you.

You need to think of what you can do to improve the lives of others, to earn self-fulfilment and life satisfaction. You do not need to be affluent to start this. Life is not all about money. This is simply a noble goal, trying to figure out what you can do to make others happy, so that they will earn a positive impact from you. Your desire to impact positively on others brings out the best in you. This equally translates to your being able to unlock the great potential in you, and this will equip you with the power of love and respect from others.

What Can You Offer?

You have to find out what gives you joy and extend that to others. You may be a great organiser, a wonderful public speaker, a nice cook, a humourist, a computer operator, a fashion designer, and so on. Your services can be rendered freely to make a positive impact. However, before such services could be rendered, be pretty sure that they are your identified skills and talents. Equally of note is that they should be what you truly enjoy doing, so that you will be able to consistently offer the assistance. If you are a student, you can offer to organise a study group before your exam, or offer to lend out your notes to those who could not attend lessons/lectures with you. If you are a teacher, let other teachers gain from your experiences in your course or area of specialisation. A person in your neighbourhood may be in dire need of operating a computer or lessons or maybe just another service. The proper thing to do is to offer your services, especially if you have the ability to do so. When you notice downcast situations around you, a little sense of humour can rekindle the lost joy. Your catering services may be beneficial to a neighbour who is organising an event. Your tailoring services can be freely offered to indigent children around you.

If you are an affluent person in the society, you need to think of ways to impact your community. You can sponsor several community projects or help the downtrodden of your society. If you decide to stretch your benevolence to a school, you can consider sponsoring programmes like inter-house sports competitions, cultural activities, talent hunts, and so on. You can equally enrich their libraries with relevant materials like books, magazines, and Compact Disc plates (for storage of materials that have soft copies).

To draw this point home, an example comes to mind here in the personage of Dr Ifeanyi Uba, the Managing Director of Capital Oil and Gas Ltd. The love he gets from people is not as a result of his wealth; after all, there are several other wealthy men who are despised. The people's affection for Dr. Uba is due to the positive impact he is making on society. He is generally known for his selfless service and generosity. These attributes have endeared countless people to him. He has sponsored many activities and programmes such as sports development, engagement in humanitarian activities to help the less privileged, establishment of industrial parks, sponsorship of a football club, employment generation, scholarship scheme, and so on. Dr. Uba equally touches people spiritually through donations towards God's work and projects. He commits to spiritual developmental strides irrespective of which religion or denomination is involved. What I have observed in his actions is encapsulated in Anne Frank's saying: "No one has ever become poor by giving."[5] As one gives, one gets more. This is the secret of prosperity which he has imbibed. This is a worthy virtue that can catapult one to enviable greatness.

There are many other services people can offer. Those who have the wherewithal should look for children from indigent parents, to adopt. This is a way of giving those children the opportunity of benefitting from their wealth. They should not concentrate on training only their own children. They can get a child from a poor family whose parents find it difficult to train, and incorporate into their own family circle. They should let the child enjoy all that their own children are enjoying – academic life, social life, moral life, financial life, and so on. They will bring up that child as their own until he or she becomes independent. By so doing, they are living a purposeful life, and a life of fulfilment. They should not make the mistake of doing it for them to be appreciated, because it may not always be so, but they should do it for the sake of impacting positively on humanity. What else can be better than sacrificial love, since we are bound to sacrifice certain pleasures, to ensure that others have a share of what we have? It is important to state that getting such a child should not translate to a case of maltreating such a child as some people would do, turning such a child into a slave. Every child is worthy of affection and should be loved totally.

Those who may not be able to incorporate the child into their own families can offer to take up the child's educational needs or other types of social support such as skill acquisition, provision of jobs, sponsorship in one type of programme or the other. One comedian used to cite this expression: "If you eat alone, you die alone." This sounds funny, but makes a lot of sense. When we make our special services available to others, we can be considered to be making a positive impact.

Are You Impacting On Others?

Several people have made a true and real impact in the world around them. That is not to say that they are privileged, advantaged, or 'special' in any way, but that they have crushed circumstances surrounding their initial limited capabilities, and found ways to pick themselves up and rise above their circumstances, to transform their own lives and the lives of those around them. By engaging with people in open, mutually beneficial ways, you are impacting positively on them. You will push beyond any introversion, shyness, or reluctance, to relate well with others, and build mutually-supportive relationships that catapult both parties to a higher level. You will dedicate yourself to what gives your life meaning and purpose. You will need to find that there is a purpose for your life, and that purpose usually involves some aspects of turning your 'mess' into a 'message', or using what you have learnt — often the hard way — as a means of being of service to others.

There is the call for you to spread what you know. Those who make a true positive difference cannot help but share and teach what they have learnt. They see their success story as information that has to be shared with the world, for its betterment. You should believe that your ideas and innovations are of use and value to others, so, you need to share them openly, and teach others what you have learnt. You have to live up to the principle of 'the more you give, the more you get'. Use your power and influence well. Those who impart the world for the better are careful and judicious with their words, actions and behaviour. You need to take your gifts seriously, as a special honour and responsibility, not to be flaunted or misused. Ensure that you understand your role and accept it with grace, compassion and care.

Making a positive impact involves showing respect to others. Whether you are successful or powerful, you should not step on others to get ahead. Do not take people for granted. Uplift others as you ascend. You will always have the urge for others to grow, unlike some power mongers who are cruel to their subordinates. If you really want to impact positively on others, your ultimate goal should not be about upholding your title, income, reputation, status or power, but about new ways to help and share with others.

For people to be positively impacted by you, you have to admit when you make mistakes, and apologise accordingly. Nobody is perfect. When you make a mistake, people around you need to know that you made a mistake, then move ahead and correct it. This move will help them understand that everyone makes mistakes, and that you can make it right. The junior ones imbibe this virtue from you, and that makes the world a better place. It is often the little things you do that make the difference in the way children perceive how to succeed in business and relationships.

While in school, for example, a student can make positive impact by joining a club in the school, using it as a medium to raise the standard of the school, and also to train other students in the area of affective domain. Through debating club too, a gifted student can equally influence other students on learning how to talk convincingly, casting away unnecessary shyness and timidity. A practical illustration of how a student can raise the standard of the school, in order to win laurels, is as shown in the Nigerian movie, *Nkoli nwa Nsukka*. Nkoli, the central character of the movie, has to coach the other students in dancing practice. This is in a bid to ensure that the school wins in a competition they are slated to participate in. She does this to great result as the school wins the competition eventually. She makes a positive impact on both the other students and the entire school, because, through the victory, the school's standard is raised. A great lesson should be learnt here of what commitment, leadership and dedication can bring to people. This is aside from the entertainment value of the movie which, of course, is another area of positive impact through the ease of tension by viewers, as they laugh and derive joy from such.

Making an effort to befriend a new student who has not yet understood the rigours of the school will avail the new student the opportunity to get good orientation on the rules and regulations of the school. This is a positive impact. When a student in the school takes time to coach a classmate who is struggling with a particular subject, that student is making a difference positively. This can bring about an improvement in the general result of a school, especially in external examinations[6]. Teachers can also impact positively on students through demonstration of mastery of their subjects, response to students' personal interests or talents, improvisation of measures to meet a particular student's need, and maintenance of admirable standards. Everyone needs to impact positively on his environment.

Spread Joy

"There is no joy like spreading joy!" goes a popular saying. Joy is not a rare material simply found in material things, money, or positions alone. It is a gift that lies in us all. We need to look inwards, do things that give us happiness and smiles that translate to joy. All we need to do with our acquired or derived joy is to share it with others. Joy is a strange thing that only increases as you spread it. In essence, the more generous you are with spreading or giving out joy, the more it will be multiplied for you. The only way truly to have great joy is to give joy. When you spread joy, your heart will be flooded with great joy. We can spread joy around us, at work, at school, with our children, with our parents, with our friends and with strangers on the street. When others are talking, you have to give a listening ear as this makes them feel good. You are indirectly spreading joy, by giving a listening ear. It shows you care about other people's thoughts.

You can spread joy by giving a huge honest smile to someone. Your smile can make all the difference in the world. That little smile makes you attractive, and makes someone else happy. Smiling shows people that you are a positive person, and that you are easy to get along with. It is the most welcoming gesture. Greet someone cheerfully. A little 'hello' sends joy to the person you are greeting. Do not hoard your greetings. Practising cheerful greetings earns you joy. Mere hugging of someone around you gives the person a feeling of intimacy with you. The person will feel accepted. This is a common practice when one reunites with a loved one. But that joy can equally be shared with others.

You can spread joy through genuine compliments. Naturally, when someone receives compliments from another person, he or she feels high in spirit. That brings joy to the recipient. We do not have to be miserly in paying compliments to others. Their morale needs to be boosted. There is great joy in receiving compliments.

Try to surprise someone with small presents, and you will make that person's day. Open hands, they say, bring open doors. Everyone has something he or she is endowed with, to positively impact others. A good way to surprise others and make great positive impact is to assist the indigent students. You can do this through purchasing books for them, paying their school fees, providing jobs for the ones who have completed schooling, and equipping them with what it takes to have a worthy living. You can equally offer assistance to a stranger. When you do that to someone who was not initially expecting a help from you, you have made yourself a hero to that person, having given him joy for that act you performed.

When you settle down to count your blessings, you will see every reason why you should strive to make positive impact on your environment. You may have had the advantage of fulfilling your career, but, what about others who could not have such opportunity? For the adults, there are as many opportunities as possible, for you to bring about positive changes in other people's lives, on a daily basis, no matter how small. You, as a child, may be identified with running errands for the elderly, or offering some minor social services to people, without looking for gratification. You are spreading joy through that, and God will make you great for doing that. When we spread joy, we earn joy.

Your Attitude Crowns It All

Attitude to life is the ultimate watchword for everyone, no matter our travails or opportunities. As Charles R. Swindle, an author, educator, and radio preacher, observed: "The longer I live, the more I realise my impact of attitude on life. Attitude, to me, is more important than facts. It is more important than the past, than education, than money, than circumstances, than failures, than successes, than what other people think or say or do. It is more important than appearance, giftedness, or skill. It will make or break a company… a church….a home. The remarkable thing is we have a choice every day regarding the attitude we will embrace for that day. We cannot change the inevitable. The only thing we can do is play on the one string we have, and that's our attitude…..I am convinced that life is 10% what happens to me, and 90% how I react to it. And so it is with you…..we are in charge of our Attitudes." The determining factor that leads us to our desired success is our attitude.

Being really practical about having a positive attitude to life, and equally, impacting positively on other people's lives, needs to be stressed here. There are people who will so much impact positively on you that you can never allow their names to be swept away from your sweet memories. These are people who have, through their humanitarian gestures, demonstrated what it means to appreciate other people's existence. Worthy of mention here is the practical demonstration of this attribute by Professor (Mrs) Julie Okpala, who has shown me tender care, real gentleness, pure humility, motherly concern, true Godly worship, deep friendship, and above all, positive attitude to life.

Through her impact on my life, I was able to build more resilience, more love for others, and more spirit of determination, as she morally encouraged me when I was writing some pages of this book in her London residence. Though she is a professor of Geographic & Environmental Education she has equally delved into many other areas of human development and concern, through her researches in some areas ravaging mankind. Of particular interest to me is the book she wrote on diabetes, which is a step towards salvaging humanity from this deadly ailment. After an experience she had, she decided to write on the topic: *Degrading Diabetes: My Personal Experience,* just to get others informed. Due to her concern for leaving no stone unturned in her findings, she took serious time to visit hospitals and relevant offices, link the internet services, make personal contacts with specialist doctors, make thorough researches on relevant books, to unravel the best ways of dissociating oneself from this dreadful ailment, diabetes.

The book, with the full research made on the contents, is a masterpiece by my estimation. This step really motivated me, as this has made a serious impact on me in my literary career. As a means of encouragement, she was always quick to ask me – continuously – in her sweet and gentle voice: "Uche, how are you getting on with the writing of your book?" I am really happy for that inspiration and sincere encouragement. She is a great and wonderful lady!

What about you? Who can boast of you as having made a positive impact on him or her? You may not know the weight of gratitude the recipient of your goodwill may have, until you see it demonstrated by that person in one way or the other. On the other hand, if you are the one that got the positive impact, it pays to show gratitude, be it in print or otherwise. You are equally indirectly impacting positively on the person you are thanking, because, gratitude is a great morale booster. That is how each and every one of us will make the world a better place. Check yourself thoroughly and adjust, where necessary. It will do you real good to have a positive attitude towards life, so that you will be assured of a firm bridge between problems and solutions.

~ Touch Me Once Again ~

1. What a sweet and sincere contact
Devoid of being artificial
And enriched with positive impact
Quite proven to be beneficial.

2. Out of your own goodwill,
I'm rising to my greatness
My aim in life to fulfil,
And gazing at its brightness.

3. I'm provided with the stool
To display all the mastery
And never to play the fool,
While I unravel life's mystery.

4. You do not mind your position
And qualitative repute
But still honour my ambition
This gesture, will I salute.

5. I'm touched by your compliment
Which you do not withhold
May you truly be prominent
As your great deeds unfold.

Chapter 6
Creative Thinking

Creativity is a phenomenon whereby something new and valuable, is created. This may be an idea, a joke, a literary work, painting, or musical composition, a solution, an invention, and so on. It is characterised by expressiveness, and imagination. When we are in an optimal state of mind for generating new ideas, we are already involved in creative thinking. This involves our ability to maximise the ability of the brain to think of new ideas. You should trust your imagination because there is always something in the box. Being creative is a strong way to make progress in unfolding what is in you.

Discover Yourself

You need to know who you are before you can effectively harness your creative abilities. By knowing yourself concretely, and accepting your personality, you will be inspired to generate an idea, after imagining and improving on it. After this, you will be motivated, through self-confidence you have built, to go on with the execution of your idea.

Creativity can be developed through establishing purpose and intention, building basic skills, encouraging acquisitions of domain-specific knowledge, stimulating and rewarding curiosity and exploration. It can equally be developed through motivation, especially internal motivation, encouraging confidence, and a willingness to take risks, focusing on mastery, and promoting supportable beliefs about creativity. Development of creativity can also be done by providing opportunities for choice and discovery, developing self-management, teaching techniques and strategies for facilitating creative performance.

You need to initiate ideas on your own through imagination and innovation. Depending completely on other people's works makes you lose your originality. If you are able to conceive, compose, invent, originate, produce, and initiate new ideas, thoughts, and physical objects, then you are on the path of creativity. You have to groom yourself better, in order to achieve your goal. The use of ingenuity sets your ball rolling. This quality of being cleverly inventive or resourceful will definitely oust you from treacherous circumstances and intimidating situations. The general idea is that you can use your ideas to improve on situations or what you are doing. Creativity does not say undoing a particular thing but bringing your own way of creating a solution.

No Pain, No Gain

Life is full of risks. Without pain, there is no gain. Denis Waitley, one of the most respected keynote lecturers and productivity consultants in the world, warns us by stating that life is inherently risky. There is only one big risk we should avoid at all costs, and that is the risk of doing nothing. Equally, Aristotle, the Ancient Greek philosopher, affirms that there is only one way to avoid criticism, and that is by doing nothing, saying nothing and being nothing. Definitely, you will not wish to settle for nothing. We should not worry about failures, but worry about the chances we miss when we don't even try. If you avoid pain, you will never reach a professional level as a body builder. There is great reward value for the price of hard work.

Suffering is necessary sometimes to make progress. For you to improve, you must be diligent, be committed to making progress and hardworking, even to the point where it hurts. Take for instance, a student who is aiming to get high grades without commensurate work and study, is merely planning to fail. Workers who wish to get promoted and get recommendations, without full dedication to their duties, are just wasting their time. The practical example used by our trainers during physical exercises to see that we put in much effort to reduce the calories we have in our bodies in order to be fit, is an eye opener that nothing good comes easy. Just remember that if you can dream it, you can do it. Be a champion today because champions do not quit.

Don't Be A Daydreamer

We must all strive to have at least a chance — a positive one — in our lives, to show that we really exist. Stephen Covey, an American educator, author, businessman, and keynote speaker, stated thus: "Ineffective people live day after day with unused potential. They experience synergy in small, peripheral ways in their lives. But creative experiences can be produced regularly, consistently, almost daily, in people's lives. It requires enormous personal security and openness and a spirit of adventure." We should learn to be creative. You can make something out of nothing.

Having a fantastic, impractical idea will simply make you run away from the obvious. You should not remain a daydreamer. Thomas Merton, an Anglo-American author of French origin, was right to observe that a daydream is an evasion. Thinking of how to become a successful entrepreneur, for instance, boils down to nothing when you cannot even make a little start of a small business. Some people just sit tight on their situations, waiting for manna to fall from heaven. They remain the way they see themselves. There is no record of progression or regression. This is an unfortunate situation. This leads to criminal thoughts — going into armed robbery, kidnapping, thuggery, prostitution, and so on. However, when you choose to work with your ideas, your cherished dreams will turn to reality. Don't be a daydreamer.

Do Not Compare Yourself To Others

This is a destructive habit. Comparing yourself to others has negative effects on you, and you will definitely feel bad about yourself. By the time you compare jobs, houses, relationships, cars, popularity, bags, shoes, dresses, and so on, you will end up creating negative feelings within yourself. You are unique and simply you. "Comparison is the thief of joy", so asserts Theodore Roosevelt, the 26th President of the United States (1901-1909). It robs you of your precious time that you would have used to do something more meaningful with yourself. Negative social comparison decreases your self-esteem, and it damages your self-confidence, and makes it more difficult for you to achieve the kind of life you want.

Avoid comparisons such as: "I wish I had a very beautiful house like my friend"; "My cousin's child is more intelligent than mine"; "How I wish I had a tall father like my friend"; "My husband's brother is lucky to have a better job", and so on. We make ourselves feel bad when we compare ourselves to others whom we perceive to be more successful than we are. Mark Twain[7], who was lauded the greatest American humourist of his era, says: "Comparison is the death of joy." It is harmful to one's mental health due to the risk of depression. Comparing yourself based on other peoples success is one of the easiest ways to feel bad about oneself, so, do not get involved in that habit.

If you want people to respect you, then be content with yourself. Think of all the good qualities you have that will make you excel. You know very well that there are good qualities in you, which the others do not have. These are what should boost your ego. Rather than comparing yourself to others, simply compare yourself to yourself. That is the best practice that will give you mental peace and contentment. How do you do this? - By assessing yourself from time to time, to see how far you have come, the changes you have effected in your life, the obstacles you have overcome, and the achievements you have made. That will really make you feel good about yourself, and will motivate you to look for more grounds to cover.

Develop A Positive Attitude To Life

Developing a positive attitude to life brings us into limelight. One who feels dejected and rejected finds it difficult to think creatively. Your mental attitude to life is one of the key elements of your personality makeup. For your creative thinking to yield you positive results, you need to do what makes you happy and what is not harmful. This will, of course, stimulate you to bring out the best in you.

You should never be ashamed of how you feel. You are the proud owner of yourself so bring out the best attitude in you so that you will succeed. Ask yourself if you are really happy doing what you are doing. William E. Gladstone, Prime Minister of Great Britain on four separate occasions between 1868 and 1894, noted for his moralistic leadership, advised thus: "Be happy with what you have and are, be generous with both, and you won't have to hunt for happiness."

Positive attitude towards life yields success. A neighbour of ours at Enugu in the 80's, was known for her ever-smiling face, despite her poverty. There was never a guarantee of what her family would eat, each new day, with her five children. However, her humorous nature got her attracted to neighbours, who were competing to feed her and the children. She found delight in making other people happy, and rendering some minor services to them. Consequently, all her children's school fees were taken up by such grateful neighbours. Later on, an entrepreneur owning a big firm employed her, on the basis of her positive attitude to life. He found in her, a persevering and happy woman, who never minded the negative forces of wretchedness around her. Today, she is a force to reckon with, as she has fully established a prospering business.

Set Your Goal And Work Towards It

This gives you direction of life. When this is done, you are motivated, through self-confidence, to drive towards what is on your mind. Any journey without a destination point is an endless journey. If you know what you want to achieve, you will know where to concentrate your efforts on.

Of course, setting goals is the first thing to be done if one wishes to record achievements.

The full determination to achieve your goal is a driving force towards its realisation. Someone came to me one day and said: "I want to become an actor." That was his goal. I told him: "work towards it. You can organise some plays with your siblings, mates, neighbours, friends, and so on." He set his goal, remained focused, and worked on it. Even as he entered the higher institution, he did not relent, as he joined the dramatic club and theatre group in all the institutions he attended. He is presently doing well in the film industry. He went in and got what he wanted, because his mindset was already on acting. Focus on your goal, and you will get what you are aiming at.

Try Hard Enough

Remind yourself that things are possible when you try hard enough. There is no way you can break a palm kernel with an egg, because the egg cannot perform that job. It will surely break. You need a stone for that. In the same way, hard situations need courage and determination. Do not consider serious situations with a mere wave of the hand. Face problems squarely. You also have to work on your goals squarely for you to realise them.

When you try hard enough, you see yourself performing unusual tasks, thereby being creative. I remember the Creativity Workshop I attended sometime ago in New York City, with a sense of fulfilment on creativity. We were asked by our professors, Shelley Berc and Alejandro Fogel, to embark on an imaginary journey, closing our eyes. We found ourselves on an imagination spree. We were told to visualise our grandmothers in a dream, handing over an inexplicable item to us, in that dream. In the assumed journey, we were meant to see some obstacles like monsters, trying to snatch the strange gifts from us. Suddenly, we were asked to open our eyes, and recount, in writing, all that transpired within that dream journey.

We were equally asked to suggest how we would make use of that strange gift given to us by our grandmothers. Not only were we asked to write them down, we were equally asked to make artistic impressions of all that we saw, including our grandmothers' pictures, the treasure pot, the monster, the trees on the way, possible streams we crossed to reach the other side of the world, the road paths we took, and so on. Oh!!! What an assignment! For me, I didn't know how to draw. But we were encouraged to try hard enough, at least to start scribbling something. We boldly took pencil and paper. Wow! I was surprised to see what I could eventually draw and write. That was real creativity at work, as I started drawing and focusing on getting a meaningful result. I finally came up with some meaningful impressions. An adage that one cannot pass hard faeces with an unserious face is applicable here. You just have to tighten your face, for you to be able to push out that 'hard nut' blocking your anus. The journey may be rough, but the end is always smooth.

Support Creativity

Teaching students to solve problems that do not have well-defined answers is one of the ways a teacher uses to boost creativity on the part of students. The students will be compelled to find the correct answers through their own resourcefulness. Students will equally make great use of their minds when they are made to create and design certain things by themselves. Such opportunities enable them manufacture things like clocks, radios, fans, chairs, tables, and so on. Their products will be showcased when schools organise periodic exhibitions. This act motivates students to be more creative. It is always exciting to discover how creative students can be when they are given the chance. It is during such functions that school authorities discover the capability of students in being creative. Such should be encouraged, so that the potentials in these young ones will be fully unlocked.

In the offices, too, the staff should be enabled to show their creative prowess. Some of them are, unfortunately, being underrated. Some of the staff have the ability of recycling some products, for better use. Some are wizards in computer work. They only need to be supported. Equally, at home, the children are talented in one way or the other. If you notice that a particular child is very good in drawing, for instance, you have to support and encourage him by buying the needed poster colours, drawing boards, pencils, erasers, and so on, to motivate him to showcase his creativity. Our support goes a long way.

Creative Thinking Does You Good

It is worthwhile to engage in creative thinking because you will have an edge over your mates. Success will be easily achieved. When you are creative, you will increase your earning power. There is no way you can be complaining of lack of funds, because, you can generate that through creative thinking. You will make a positive difference through creative thinking. It will not be *'business as usual'*, because you will be distinguished from others, and you will equally earn respect. You will struggle less, and achieve more, due to creative thinking. When your brain is at work, your achievements are bound to be great. Since you already know the ways to get on with what intention you have, you will struggle less.

Being creative makes you happy. You have the freedom to express yourself in ways you feel is best for you. Self-confidence is increased through creativity. When you do something new and succeed, definitely, you will be more confident in yourself. Your mental aspects of life will be enhanced, due to the fact that you will be mentally alert to respond to situations. Your spirit will equally be positively high for your creative endeavours.

Many organisations record very low productivity because of their slow and difficult ways of solving problems; but through creative thinking, you will recognise and solve problems quicker and easier. Surely, through creativity, you will become a voice for innovation. You can be called at any time to come up for one new idea or the other. You will enjoy greater job satisfaction. When your colleagues are struggling to understand their problems, you are fully satisfied with what you are doing, because you are resourceful enough to tackle your problems. Your creative thinking speeds up your career advancement. This is because your mind is always preoccupied with what actions you will take to enhance your career. You will always be ahead of others.

~ Unstoppable In My Creativity ~

1. As I'm going through my imagination
And thinking of an innovation
I'm stepping up with great confidence
To move into prominence.

2. The crave for originality
Has brought about ingenuity
To unlock that great potential
With the needed credential.

3. I cannot but appreciate
The golden chance to initiate
A worthwhile creativity
In my own dear nativity.

4. Walking with real motivation
To the realm of affirmation
Never to opt for sinking
But go for creative thinking.

5. I have to be truly unstoppable
In what seems to be attainable
As I earnestly move on gradually
To reach the peak, successfully.

Chapter 7
Build On Your Mistakes

To err is human; to forgive is divine', goes a popular saying. A mistake is an error in action, calculation, opinion, or judgement, caused by poor reasoning, carelessness, insufficient knowledge, and so on. It is equally a misunderstanding or misconception. One big problem with some people is that they take failures or making mistakes as the end of life. It helps to realise that as humans, we will definitely make mistakes and when we do, we have to move on. The issue does not lie in making mistakes, but on learning from the mistakes made, and consequently, building on them. Success comes after the realisation of our mistakes. It is like the saying "Success comes through rapidly fixing our mistakes, rather than getting things right the first time."

One of the most recognised and influential pastors in the world, Rick Warren, reminded us that we are products of the past, but that we don't have to be prisoners of it. Equally, Albert Einstein[8], the German-born American physicist, Nobel laureate, and most famous scientist of the 20th century, whose greatest brainchild was the Theory of Relativity, and who discovered the hugely important and iconic equation, $E = mc^2$, clearly asserted that: "Anyone who has never made a mistake has never tried anything new." We should note that the word 'correction' would not have existed if there were no mistakes.

No One Is Above Mistakes

No one is above mistakes; therefore, we are all bound to make mistakes at one time or the other. I remember when I was very young, my father, through his actions, made us think that fathers could not make mistakes. If anyone mistakenly hit a chair, he would ask the question: "Can't you look?" But, if he was the one who mistakenly hit the chair, the question would turn to: "Who kept this chair here?" He was simply trying to defend his ego. The fact was that he did not want us to make the same mistakes, but mistakes, we should know, are inevitable even if they do look avoidable sometimes.

Another experience of people not acknowledging their mistakes was when I was in primary school. It was during an English lesson. Our teacher was writing on the chalkboard, and spelt one word wrongly. I innocently pointed it out to him, but, rather than acknowledging the mistake and correcting it, he told me to shut up. I felt demoralised and confused, because I was sure of what I was pointing out to him. His reason for telling me to shut up was quite obvious – he did not want us, the pupils, to believe that he could ever be wrong. What an obsession!

Incidentally, this is still happening in some schools today. Teachers should own up their mistakes and let the pupils know that they are equally human beings, just as the pupils are. Let the pupils understand that when one makes a mistake, he or she should try to correct it. In the offices too, some bosses can never admit that they are making mistakes, or that they are wrong. They are always 'Mr. Right' or 'Mrs. Right', and that is why people dare not proffer useful advice, for them to function more effectively. Do not forget that two heads are better than one. It takes a second person to point out your mistake, and you just have to acknowledge it. After all, no one is perfect.

Corrections Are Needed

This is one of the reasons educationists insist that children in schools should do corrections on failed areas, before any new subject matter can be effectively handled. I have never heard that it is possible to count number two before counting number one. This is a very serious deal in the school system.

It does not matter the way and manner you may wish to correct the wrong notion, but let the right answers be proffered. A teacher who wrongly gives an answer to the students in the class owes them the responsibility to go back and correct that mistake; otherwise, the children will grow with the wrong stuff in their brains. It is a common thing that our egos become our worst enemies when it comes to failing. We are tempted to do what we can to save our faces, but unfortunately, this wreaks havoc on us, because the result is not productive.

Mistakes Are Challenges

When a mistake is made, it gives you the opportunity of reassessing your action, with a view to correcting the errors. This, consequently, challenges you to improve and get the correct result. A student, for example, who fails in an examination, has the obligation to build on the mistake made, in order to succeed next time. You just need to challenge the *status quo* of your own making. Since others could make it, you too, can make it. That mistake now becomes a challenge.

In the area of politics, it is not the end of life for a politician to lose an election. The politician, through the loss, will have the opportunity to critically examine himself, to know areas of amendment in his or her political life. When that self-realisation is gotten, he will be on a smoother terrain of the race next time he makes an attempt. Stop chasing the losses, and gain more ground.

Mistakes Pave Way For Improvement

In all spheres of life, there are opportunities for people to build on their mistakes. A civil engineer can improve on the quality of building he has been delivering; a teacher can improve on his instructional approach which the students have been complaining of; a spouse can redirect his/her thought on how to correct the past mistakes of their marital life; a government official can build on the errors he has been making in the office; people in the entertainment industry can equally improve in their performances, through building on their mistakes.

For you to successfully build on your mistakes, you should explore more ideas with various new approaches, noting that failure is common. You need to recognise where you have not done well, because it is disastrous for one not to know what is wrong, or if he is wrong. The saying that "he who does not know, and does not know that he does not know, is a fool," is a reasonable saying. Cast away fears, and detach yourself emotionally so that you will be able to look at the advantage of moving further from where you are.

One essential factor of getting yourself back on track is through feedback. You need to reach out to people to get their thoughts on a particular idea. You can reach them physically or through social media, to get the comments by such people on certain ideas. By so doing, you are paving way for improvement.

Trial And Error

The constant fact in life is the issue of trial and error. By trying and making mistakes, and having one correcting oneself, he or she eventually gets to the right answer. All the electronic gadgets we are enjoying today are products that went through many mistakes, before they came to perfection.

The most effective approach for innovation is through trial and error. Sir Isaac Newton, a celebrated master of Astronomy, Chemistry, Mathematics, Physics, and Theology, went through thick and thin, to arrive at perfection. He is regarded as one of the foremost scientific intellectuals of all time, an English physicist and mathematician, most famous for his law of gravitation. Before the final invention of electric light bulbs we are using today, Thomas Alva Edison had his challenges. Many other inventors who went through challenges and series of mistakes include: George Stephenson, who invented the first Locomotive Engine; Bill Gates, who helped invent MS-DOS, which later developed into the Windows OS, which became the system used in Windows 98, 99, ME, 2000 and XP.

Equally worthy of mention are Alexander Bain, who invented the first electrical clock and fax machine; Blaise Pascal, who invented the mechanical calculator; James Maxwell, who presented the first durable colour photograph and the concept of electromagnetic theory. If these renowned technocrats did not build on their initial mistakes, they would not have come up with the concepts they are known for, today.

Acknowledge Your Mistakes

If you accept full responsibility for your mistake, rather than blaming others, you are on the sure way to building on your mistake, and heading towards success. Blaming others for your mistake is very wrong, and it creates tension wherever this is practised. You will not, consequently, be able to recognise the real problem.

Strong leadership can only be demonstrated through holding yourself accountable for your mistakes. By so doing, you are projecting yourself positively, and this will earn you enormous respect. Sharing your mistakes, with others, will enable you uncover them, for the benefit of the growth of your company or other members of your family, as they will help identify where you may have gone wrong. With the acceptance of the other people's perspective about the situation, and their consequent advisory role, you are better off.

Be A Team Player

In order to effectively build on your mistakes, you have to be a real team player. You should possess the ability to work well with others, because there is strength in unity. You cannot do everything alone. Involve others. If you take advantage of a group's collective energy and creativity, the team can accomplish much more in less time.

Having the skills to work together with your co-workers is part of being successful at work. This will help you develop worthwhile relationships with co-workers. In every aspect of life, teamwork is wonderful, and produces great result. In football, for instance, it is never possible for one person to pass the ball, blow the whistle, and be a goalkeeper. Various people are involved, and each person assists the other one to pass on to another one, who may eventually score goals for the team.

Teamwork is a vital way of completing projects that are worth developing. This can have a major impact on your career. If you are a valuable team member, there is the likelihood of having more career opportunities. Being a team player gives you and your team members the opportunity to share what you already know, analyse the situation, and then, decide on what needs to be done. In the school system, team teaching enables each person to teach the aspect he knows best in a particular subject. Being a team player involves being co-operative, dependable, and adaptable. You should learn to listen, and equally, be an effective contributor.

Teamwork makes the dream work. In leadership, it does a great work, because effective leaders do not act solely as individuals. If you realise that the purpose of a leader is to work with people to find solutions that work best collectively, then you will imbibe team play in your leadership style. Leaders are meant to bring people together. Studies have shown that the best leaders do not act with a sense of superiority; they act with a sense of empathy.

Make Use Of Support Groups

One of the effective ways of building on your mistakes is to use the services of some support groups like mentors, counsellors, advisers, who can provide you with guidance you may need to deal with the mistake. Unfortunately, some chief executives feel too proud to make use of the counsellors attached to them. This causes much damage to those organisations, as no one can advise on what is best for the growth of such organisations, schools, offices, or industries. Let it be stated here that their advice does not, in any way, undermine your authority. It will rather enhance your personality as 'one who has a listening ear.'

Every quality leader has a purpose. He needs to be passionate about what he does. Without enthusiasm, he will lack success in that profession. Knowing well that his employees look up to him for extensive field knowledge, as well as his ability to take risks and move forward, he is bound never to dismiss his mistakes as just an error. When he understands how to learn from his shortcomings, he will strive for perfection and definitely, success will be the end result. Be guided.

The Good News

The good news in Nigeria in the area of improvement can be cited in the local manufacturing of vehicles, by Innoson Vehicle Manufacturing Co. Ltd. With the improvement of some initial concepts, the company has grown tremendously. Innoson Vehicle Manufacturing Company (IVM) is the first indigenous motor manufacturing company in Nigeria and is a world class company. They manufacture buses, Sports Utility Vehicles (SUV's), trucks, pick-up vans, and cars. The visionary chairman, Dr Innocent Chukwuma, is a resourceful and accomplished entrepreneur and has been able to come up with a company that carries out optimisation design and assembly as to produce suitable products at affordable prices. He used the auto company to boost the Nigerian economy as well as generate employment.

The Innoson Group equally comprises of Technical and Industrial Co. Ltd. which produces very high quality plastic products in the country. These are various types of plastic chairs, drums, plates, jerry cans and tables with high quality. They also specialise in the manufacture of quality motorcycles and parts. The Innoson Tyre Manufacturing Company produces premium tyres that most car owners buy. The Chairman, Dr Innoson Chukwuma, has consequently empowered many Nigerian youths in the area of skill acquisition and employment. This aspect of touching people's lives stands him tall in the society. The secret behind this huge success lies in his ability to build and improve on what he originally started.

For the mineral drinks, attempts have been made by the various stakeholders to improve on them, for the greater acceptability by the populace. The mistakes that were made in the past are being worked on, and better products have emerged in the market. Some ingredients that were not suitable for the body system are now being replaced with nutrients that the body requires. A great improvement is being made, thereby building great confidence on the consumers.

Interestingly, at the national level, the move to 'rebrand the country' as a result of mistakes made in the past, was made by the then Minister of Information, Professor (Mrs.) Dora Akunyili, of blessed memory. Due to the previous bad image associated with Nigeria and her people, as a result of fraudulent acts of few Nigerians at home and abroad, there was a call that Nigeria needed image rebranding, to help change the perception of outsiders, and even some Nigerians. This programme aimed at value re-orientation and attitudinal change. This move was made to ensure that we did not continue to wallow in the thoughts of the past mistakes, but to think positively towards moving the country forward.

Another Chance For You

At every level or point in life, there is the need to correct the mistakes already made. Until we do that, there is no way one can move forward to record success. As Mary Pickford, a Canadian-American motion picture actress, a significant figure in the development of film acting, and the first star of

American cinema, advised: "If you have made mistakes, even serious ones, there is always another chance for you. What we call failure is not the falling down, but the staying down."

If you grow with the feeling that your mistake is your failure, then regard that attitude as the mistake, not the error you committed. It is only when you challenge what you feel is perfect that you can be regarded as progressing. Rather than visualising a mistake as a problem and feeling defeated, you just need to challenge yourself and those around you, to see it as an opportunity to continue to innovate. If you mistakenly fall down from a slippery staircase, then you will develop a new strategy of managing a staircase with floor tiles. You will equally develop more carefulness in using the bathtub. These are similar circumstances.

In whatever angle you deal with issues, either in business, or academics, or office work, you need to embrace your mistakes as learning experiences, and build on what you have learned, to move forward, minimise damage, and even prevent them from happening again. Let us be guided by the fact that mistakes lead us to the pathway of creating a better future for ourselves.

~ A Great Lesson ~

1. Identified formerly as a prisoner
    But later emerging as a winner
    Your own mistakes, you forsake
    In rightful thinking, you partake.

2. Focusing on your real need
    Will distance you from all greed
    Using genuine type of approach
    Will not draw you to reproach.

3. Forgetting about the past
    Will not make you come last
    As you enhance your performance
    With the necessary conformance.

4. Following the clear directive
    Will give you the right perspective
    Bearing in mind that minor error
    Can never be a terror.

5. Pursuing the ultimate amendments
    Following the stated commandments
    Drives away the entire commotion
    And ushers in your promotion.

Chapter 8

Identify With Success

S uccess is a favourable and prosperous termination of attempts or endeavours, an attainment of higher social status, achievement of a goal, honours, or the like. It is a positive achievement that every average person would like to identify with. It is a sweet experience to have. The great virtue of always being happy is through identification with it. Identifying with success comes with a lot of joy because it is a sure way to progress. It comes after some hurdles must have been crossed. That goes to say that, anyone desiring it should be ready to work towards that. You cannot just buy it.

If you wish to succeed, you should determine not to fail. This is a sure way to success. Evan Esar, an American humourist, who devoted his life to writing and compiling books of humour, stated: "Success is the good fortune that comes from aspiration, perspiration, and inspiration." Your commitment to the process of achieving your goal will lead you to success. Many people fail because of lack of determination to succeed. They did not try hard enough to disentangle themselves from failure. When you identify with success, you will definitely succeed.

Who Is Successful?

There are many ways through which we experience success. Unfortunately, some people do not acknowledge that they are successful simply because they feel that they have not acquired massive wealth. Most of the time, people express the feelings of failure. When they are succeeding, they do not feel that, because, they ignore certain little things that are positively happening in their lives. Why is it that it is only when you buy the most expensive car that you feel you are successful? Some think it is only when they build and live in a mansion in the city centre that they can be counted as being successful. Far from that! There are many other things in your life that indicate success.

You are successful when, for instance, you refuse to be a victim. When you realise that you are a co-creator of your life experiences, you will refuse to be kept down. You will keep your heads up. When you do not care what other people think, you are successful. Since you cannot please everyone, you will just keep true to yourself, and love the person you are. If your relationship with people, like your spouse, your children, your parents, your co-staff, for instance, is getting better, then, you are successful.

Successful people have empathy and love for others. So, when you find yourself spreading love and positive energy into the world, regard yourself as being successful. Some people have been able to assist others in some ways or areas. If you see that the people you assisted are doing well, count yourself as having succeeded.

If you have goals that are passionate to you and you are pursuing them, this excitement drives your life. This is characteristic of successful people, so, you are one. The realisation of the fact that you have passions that you pursue is a clear indication that you are successful, because you have been able to locate your unique talents and gifts, and you can now pursue them.

If you accept that you cannot change the things in life, but that you can change your negative perspective on situations to a positive one, then, you can be regarded as being successful. The fact that you see yourself not complaining too much is an indication of success for you. This means that you have transcended to the status of expressing gratitude. As life is full of disappointments, the moment you choose to see them as learning opportunities, and look on the bright side, you are successful.

One great inspirational quote on success, by Bessie Anderson Stanley, an American poet and author of the poem *Success*, is very encouraging here. It states: "He has achieved success who has lived well, laughed often, and loved much; who has enjoyed the trust of pure women, the respect of intelligent men and the love of little children; Who has filled his niche and accomplished his task; Who has never lacked appreciation of Earth's beauty or failed to express it; Who has left the world better than he found it; Whether an improved poppy, a perfect poem, or a rescued soul; Who has always looked for the best in others and given them the best he had; Whose life was an inspiration; Whose memory a benediction."

Work Towards Success

You need to work towards success. Swami Vivekananda, a spiritual genius of commanding intellect and power, said: "Take up one idea. Make that one idea your life - Think of it, dream of it, and live on that idea. Let the brain, muscles, nerves, and every part of your body be full of that idea, and just leave every other idea alone. This is the way to success." As a way of identifying with success, you should have the right mindset, seek opportunities, identify your strengths and weaknesses, prepare and take action. These are the skills to equip you for the opportunity you are seeking, in order to get better career. I strongly agree with Wayne Dyer, an internationally renowned author and speaker in the field of human development, that, "there is no scarcity of opportunity to make a living at what you love, there's only scarcity of resolve to make it happen."

People need to understand that they can actually work towards their own success, and not just honouring themselves with the credits from their relations who are successful. You can become that successful commissioner, author, minister, ambassador, administrator, governor, or even president. Your success will then attract the close identifications by your own associates. Life should not be made stagnant by you. You can change your situation, and success will be your name.

Success Is The Best Revenge For Failure

If you feel you have failed in life, there is revenge – success! Some people just feel that failure is the end of their lives, because they have not resorted to revenge. The best revenge is success. For you to succeed, your desire for success should be greater than your fear of failure.

Sometimes, we should be happy for disappointments, as they hold the key to our strife to make things work better. The most famous scientist of the 20th century, the 'Father of Modern Physics', the German-born American Philosopher of Science, who developed the general theory of relativity, and best known in popular culture for his Mass-Energy Equivalence formula $E = mc^2$ (which has been dubbed 'the world's most famous equation'), the recipient of the 1921 Nobel Prize in Physics, Albert Einstein (who we mentioned previously), inspires us through his saying: "I am thankful for all those who said 'NO' to me. It's because of them I'm doing it myself." What a pronouncement! Nothing can be more sincere than this. There is no doubt about this. Today, all over the world, that name is being revered.

Take every occurrence in your life (positive or negative) as a challenge to improve your life. Do not rest on your oars, and feel complacent with your situation, because life demands constant change from you; the only constant thing in life is change.

Detect Areas Of Interest

Be mindful of the fact that you cannot achieve success if you do not have desire for that. Parents are admonished to allow their children detect their own areas of interest, their hearts' desires in life, so that they can guide them towards success in such. A situation whereby a child is forced to do a course that does not really interest him may not attract the desired result of success. The child may end up being a nuisance to the family, and the society at large.

We have witnessed cases of children forced into the area of Medicine, simply because their parents wish to be called 'Doctor's daddy' or 'Doctor's mummy'. At the end of the academic pursuit, the children come out as unsuccessful medical personnel, due to lack of interest in such courses. The lives of patients entrusted into their medical care can only be protected by God. Some die out of carelessness of forgetting some instruments in the body, by the supposed doctor after surgery. Some die due to wrong prescriptions, and so on and so forth. However, a successful doctor is the one who truly desires to be that, and is devoted to that call. This is so in all professions. Success comes when we appreciate it and work towards it.

Rejoice With Others

There is opportunity of being rewarded with success when you are happy about people's successes. Do not be jealous of someone else's success, because it will never help you, and it will not place you in a comfortable situation. For goodness sake, congratulate a successful person, because yours is on the way.

The interesting thing about blessing others is that we end up being blessed. Share in the excitement of the excellent academic performance of your friend, the marriage engagement of your neighbour, the appointment of your relation, and so on. We have to expand our thinking to the point that we realise that other people's gains are not our losses. They have no bearing. We only need to appreciate the journey that got them there, and let it inspire us, and see that there is more than enough for us. Rejoice in others' happiness and your friends will surely enjoy your being happy with them. It is a sign that you care. They may even make you benefit from their successful situation and provide you advices, work opportunities, new acquaintances, and so on.

Reflect upon unselfish happiness. Do not be bitter about the success of your friend or relation; release that bitterness and personal anxiety, and let your joy be expressed. This is one of the secrets of success. Be wiser. The next turn could be yours!

Personality Refinement

When you achieve success, you will have a full personality refinement. Let the good in you shine in front of others. Remember that if you achieve success, you are no more your old self. You will redefine your social status in terms of manner of approach, life's perceptions, and general attitude towards others.

The mere fact that you feel you have succeeded will make you feel peculiar. By perfecting your personality, you will be able to reveal the beauty that lies within you. Since this is an external manifestation of your internal splendour, it is important for you to let people understand that beauty is not just about good looks, but the quality of life you are displaying. Be impressive in your character, since you are now successful.

Success Has Many Friends

The reason for asserting that success has many friends is obvious - it is the successful person that will attract friends, while failure loses its own friends. Naturally, success is a positive thing, while failure is negative. There is the saying that a successful man gains the good opinions of those who had no time for him before he became famous. Whereas they snubbed him or ignored him then, now, they seek his company. This is true.

I have never seen people who have boldly come out to be identified as relations to a particular mad person or beggar on the street. On the contrary, a person of influence in the society will easily be known and identified as: 'my uncle', 'my mother's younger sister', 'my childhood friend', and so on. People will affiliate with those powerful people by proclaiming thus: "The governor is my mother's younger brother"; "The president's father is a close friend of my father"; "My sister is a good friend of the First Lady"; "That actress was my childhood friend"; "The chairman was my classmate", and so on. These are claims by people, and some of them may not be true. People are just doing that for them to be identified with successful people.

The Price Of Success

What does it take to succeed? The price of success is "hard work, dedication to the job at hand, and the determination that, whether we win or lose, we have applied the best of ourselves to the task at hand," so says Vince Lombardi, one of the most successful football coaches in the history of the game.

Many seek success, but few are willing to make the necessary sacrifice in order to secure it. Studies have shown that it is not actually what you achieve, but what you become along the way, and who you help along the way that makes it so rich and rewarding. So, we need to do what is right, necessary, or required in a job, relationship, or career. And we need to do that with love, positive expectation, joy, and gratitude. We should equally be doing it with consistency, integrity, passion, resolve, and commitment. Follow the rules, and you will be successful.

~ Success, Here I Come! ~

1. Trying to defend my personality
   By putting off all contempt
   And freely unfolding high technicality
   Will bring to bear, my diligent attempt.

2. Guard me with the needed armour
   In order to jump the hurdle
   To be crowned with the desired honour
   Of getting the keys to sparkle.

3. I have to forget all anxiety
   Which are not really impressive
   But rather think of a better society
   And aspire to be progressive.

4. It is quite pleasant to ascend
   To the throne with so much love
   All my ways, I shall amend
   As I fly with success, like a dove.

5. Success is so much rewarding
   With it, I'll ever identify
   All its traits, I need to be supporting
   My efforts, I have to intensify.

Chapter 9

Share Your Experience

Sharing one's experience is one of the great ways of forging ahead in life. It is a rewarding fun because, as one shares his experience, he learns more from others and consequently, adds to the existing one. Sharing of experience opens one up to higher opportunities, as he becomes better equipped to face life challenges and fun. Some people are so selfish that they forget that iron sharpens iron. Of course, it takes two to tangle. When others do not benefit from you, of what use is your knowledge? It is only your ability to impart knowledge on others that will make you seem knowledgeable. This is by making them equally know what you know.

You are encouraged not to hoard your experience. Bring it into limelight, for others to tap from that your wealth of experience. If people such as Bill Gates, Albert Einstein, Isaac Newton, and the like, had not shared their experiences, I wonder what the world would have become. After learning from others, teach other people. That is the spirit of sharing.

The More You Teach Others, The More You Learn

I remember when I started attending computer literacy classes. Any new topic taught by my instructor gave me excitement and I was always eager to share the experience with others. The secret with this practice is that the more you teach others, the more you learn. I think that was really what made me progress in my computer work, as I was always eager to 'dish out' my new knowledge on the subject matter. I made it fun, and so, I never bordered what it took me in terms of time and materials.

In the office, some are talented in some areas more than their co-workers, and they vehemently refuse to share their knowledge, and this brings out low turnout of productivity. If everyone should bring out his own potentiality, the performance index of offices and workers therein will be very high.

For the school system, the students are always encouraged to share their knowledge through assistance to the less advantaged ones. Most of the time, it is when you assist fellow students that the remaining stuff gets manifested. You are even servicing your brain through that means. Bring out time; create study groups, whereby you will have the opportunity to share your experience with others. In the class, never attempt to hide yourself, or hoard the answer. Be brighter by showcasing what you have.

Don't Die In Silence

Some may not be as intelligent as others, and they may feel shy to share their own experiences. No! It is not the best practice. When you bring out what is in you, you will have the opportunity for improvement. Nobody can correct you when you have not yet voiced out your opinion or experience. If you feel you have a problem, share it with someone else because, 'problem shared is half-solved.'

Your experience can be a key to unlocking your neighbour's potential. This goes on to say that, through you, someone else can be empowered. The credit is yours, of course. Equally, your experience, when shared, gives another person the room to empower you. This life is not worth 'dying in silence.' What differentiates us, as human beings, from animals, is that we can reason. Therefore, a fellow human being can reason with you, and proffer solution to your problems. Shared experience reveals to you that you cannot do it all alone. Refuse to give up, but rather, confide in someone, and you are on your path to better life again.

Eleanor Roosevelt, an American Political leader and former First Lady of USA[9], encourages us thus: "The purpose of life is to live it, to taste experience to the utmost, to reach out eagerly and without fear for newer and richer experience." So, let us imbibe the practice of sharing our life's experiences, to create smoother way of handling our ventures.

A Cherished Shared Experience

I will always cherish the story my dad told us when we were growing up. He shared his experience in football, with us. As a disciplinarian, he believed in devotion to whatever course one is pursuing. He told us of his debut in football game: "My children, I was able to secure a job through football game. I used to play very well, so much so that I was seen everywhere, in the football pitch. Due to the skilful way I used to run in the field, I was nicknamed 'V-motor'[10]. We were the forces to reckon with, in those days. However, that was not the period they used to send footballers abroad, to all these great countries that these younger ones are enjoying now. I played so well that we were sent to places like Port Harcourt, Lagos and Calabar."

He continued, "We didn't go outside the country, but we put interest in that. We were committed to it. I was never found wanting during our regular practices. I was doing this at Enugu, and later, I was invited for an interview at

Lagos, to be employed in the Government Printing Press, so that I would form part of their football team."

He went on further: "I got employment immediately, because I possessed the 'skills' which were needed. Later on, I was posted to Enugu. I continued my football game there and later became the Team Manager of the defunct 'Enugu Black Rocks', which later metamorphosed into the present 'Rangers International Football Club'. So, you can see, it's through football that I got my job. You can equally excel in any area of interest, and place yourself on a smooth terrain in life." That was my sweet dad talking. He shared his experience with us, the children, and we were motivated to note that one's skill or talent could earn him great job satisfaction.

The stories he told us were fully buttressed when his demise attracted a lot of tributes from many great footballers and football fans. Great footballers like Coach Dominic Nwobodo and Coach Christian Chukwu, in their tribute to him, described him as a 'great football administrator'. They lamented that they had been deprived of the great interactions and advice they had been getting from him, (as member of Enugu Football Association). They equally recalled how they used to sit with him to discuss *Enugu Black Rocks* and *Rangers International F.C.* They equally recalled the moral and financial support he gave to most of them in the clubs then. They finally prayed that history will always remember him as "one of those great men who started, developed, and promoted football in the then Eastern Region in general, and East Central State, in particular." We, the children, now have that history about him and we are proud of him for having been identified as a great achiever. Thank God he shared his experience with us.

Touch Someone's Life Today With Your Experience

How do we share our experience with our children, our students, our job associates, our neighbours, our friends, our co-staff, and others? The experience you share with any of these people can change their lives. This may move them into changing their *modus operandi*, in order to earn success the way you have earned. Touch someone's life today by sharing your experience.

Sometimes, the experience you are sharing may be a worse situation than that of the person you are sharing with. Someone lost a child, but when she heard the story of how a family completely perished in a road accident, she calmed down, because she heard of a worse situation. Let people understand that their situations are not the worse off, by revealing worse situations to them. You are indirectly healing their wounds. We are advised that, no matter how far down we have been, we should see how our experience can help others. It is important to give back and pay it forward with sharing your knowledge and experience with others.

Business Ventures

Experienced people in a particular business tend to do better than those who are just starting. A beginner should always feel free to share his experience with the advanced ones, for them to know areas of assistance. You may be thinking that you are in the right track, not knowing you are planning to fail.

Among business men and women, there is the need for them to meet from time to time, to share their experiences. This will result in better productivity, as each person tends to ameliorate his ways of handling his business. They will even have healthier working relationships. Love will be injected into their hearts, as they proffer strategies on how to move forward. No man is an island.

Is It Worthy To Share Your Experience?

Sharing your experience with others will empower you to look back on what you have done. Most times, people do not realise the extent of progress or damage they have encountered when these experiences have not yet been shared. It is while sharing that you fully appreciate the exact thing that happened.

This gives you the opportunity to inspire others, pass on thoughts and ideas. The person you are sharing it with will say: "if this person has been able to do it, why can't I?" One instance is that of driving. If you share your experience of how you started driving and how you were filled with fear of hitting a tree or a house, and how you later overcame the fear, that will go a long way to giving hope to a learner. His proclamation, surely, will be "Yes, I can." When you share your experience, you will be enabled to use different skills, especially in presentations.

Sharing reinforces learning, and heightens your awareness. This is noteworthy, especially those who are preparing for examinations, interviews and advancement in their career prospects. This strengthens previous knowledge acquired. The moment you start sharing a particular experience, you will have the opportunity to reflect on the experience, and this gives better meaning to the experience. If it is a group work, sharing of experience will help strengthen relationship with one another. It brings about memorable occasions because the outcome is fun, as there will be shared moments, shared success, and shared adversity.

There's Fun In Sharing

Sharing makes life real. When important events come up, whether good or bad, sharing them with others makes them come to life. In fact, the easiest way to disconnect from people is to avoid sharing. But when we share with others, we have the opportunity to celebrate accomplishments, talk through difficult decisions, and treat our inner dialogue as something of value. When we realise that life is fun, and that we need to show something for it, then we begin to share ideas, problems and successes.

Each time you share with someone else, you develop a feeling of satisfaction. So, sharing feels good. You can imagine sharing the best way of solving a Mathematics puzzle with a fellow student, only for that puzzle to appear in your exam question paper. The fact that you have assisted someone in that knowledge gives you psychological satisfaction. Continue doing good. People's trust in us will surely shoot up, because we are always ready and eager to share our experiences with them. When you do not open up for someone to hear from you, how do you think that the person will trust you? It is only through your own practical demonstration of sharing, that some level of confidence will be established, for people to increase their trust in you.

When we share our experiences, the gesture makes others feel that they are not alone in such circumstances. They will come to realise that some other people have equally undergone such experiences and therefore, they will have hope of coming out of the problems. The more we share the more gratitude we bring into our lives. This is because the people we share with or assist will always be grateful. You too, will be grateful that you were privileged to share with someone else.

Many authors and psychologists have confirmed the need for sharing. As Charlotte Brontë[11], author of the classic novel, *Jane Eyre*, said: "Happiness quite unshared can scarcely be called happiness, it has no taste." Equally, Elie Wiesel, a Jewish-American professor and political activist, stated that: "Friendship marks a life even more deeply than love. Love risks degenerating into obsession, friendship is never anything but sharing." Then, our popular Brian Tracy, professional speaker, author, success expert, the most listened to radio author on personal and business success in the world today, attests: "Love only grows by sharing. You can only have more for yourself by giving it away to others."

Sharing your experience gives you the opportunity of finding your voice. You learn how to express yourself, and learn how to think about what has happened in your life, in a way that makes sense.

~ The Best Teacher ~

1. What a joy we get in sharing
    And none at all in hoarding
    If we are not so selfish
    We shall not really perish.

2. For us to come to limelight
    We need to see the sunlight
    As the land has to be flowered
    Our minds have to be powered.

3. Heavy loads, we need to lighten
    Our hearts, we have to strengthen
    From others, come assistance
    We cannot afford resistance.

4. For one to be knowledgeable
    And get things that are profitable
    It will turn out to be emptiness
    If there is no sufficient loveliness.

5. Our experiences, we must share
    To show we really care
    Our dreams, we should realise
    To ensure we stabilise.

Chapter 10
Be Yourself

Being yourself means aligning your beliefs, words, and, actions. You are the one controlling your actions. You are not depending on anyone else to dictate the pace for you, as you are simply accountable to yourself. You are not making any attempt to falsify your true self, in order to gain grounds. Rather, you are projecting your own nature. Note that there is no other you. It is not possible for you to unfold what is in you when you are not being yourself. Consequently, this is a necessary trait to possess, in order for one's gift to be his power. Ralph Waldo Emerson, one of America's greatest writers, a philosopher and essayist once said that "to be yourself in a world that is constantly trying to make you something else is the greatest accomplishment."

It baffles me the way some people falsify the personality in them. You have to reject the spirit of false life. As Alan Watts, a British-born philosopher, writer, and speaker, best known as an interpreter and populariser of Eastern philosophy for a Western audience, puts it: "Waking up to who you are requires letting go of who you imagine yourself to be." The person who is a jerk to others and the person who is afraid of social situations are both not being themselves. Their life is just being covered with conditioned, fear-based thinking.

False Identity

Sometimes, we find ourselves doing what it takes for the other person to accept us. In most cases, these actions are detrimental to our true essence, and we cannot play such role for long. We refrain from being ourselves, for fear of being rejected or unaccommodated. You do not even realise that if you are chosen by the other person under that circumstance, it is not 'you' the person has chosen, but that artificial person you claim to be. You can only imagine what happens when you go back to your normal self. Do you not feel it can be disastrous? The consequence is that you must consistently be this 'someone else' you thought you should be, to keep what the other person has given you, leading to unhappiness.

The case of revealing a false identity to people is a practical example of not being one's self. Why should one say one is a lawyer, when one is really a carpenter or petty trader? Is it because you want to 'raise' your social status? You may even fall into the hands of someone whose flair is not for lawyers, but for carpenters or traders. So, the best bet is being you.

It is due to being 'fake' that people indulge in a lot of atrocities. Align your actions with your thoughts and beliefs. Do not practise the notorious slogan of "Do what I say, but don't do what I do." Do not imagine yourself to be someone else, so that you can practically figure out the best you can do with your true self. There are those who boast of things that they are not. Putting it in context, telling other students, for example, that one's parents are always dining with Mr President; when, in essence they are finding it difficult to get a proper meal a day, will definitely block one's chances of getting help, when needed. This is not far-fetched but something that is really common among a lot of people.

There are cases where some men go to the extent of borrowing cars, in order to attract the love of the girls they wish to have a relationship with. Come on, this deceit cannot last, because, sooner or later, the truth comes out. Any reasonable person will not accept you for what you '*pose*' with, but, for what you truly are. If you show you are poor, the girl may even be the one to lift you up. The womenfolk are not left out here. Be content with how you look, so that the confidence in you will brighten you up. Why bleach your body when you know that, one day, your true complexion will manifest? Is it not better for the man who wishes to marry you to see you as that 'dark complexioned girl whom I love', than 'that fake fair-complexioned girl who deceived me'? Check yourself.

Ask yourself more: what happens when your lie fades and the person finds out the real you? Why build on a shaky foundation when your original self might be a far better bargaining power in love, work or any of life's circumstance?

Be Not Deceived

There was a man who was always giving people the wrong impression of himself. He claimed to have everything, and know every influential person in the country. He went as far as carrying stethoscope, claiming that he was a medical doctor. He was collecting money from uninformed people, and promising them that he would be able to take care of their health challenges. The man claimed he was always in touch with all the people of high influence, especially those in power. At the mention of the name of any President, Governor, or minister, this man would claim immediately that he just had a chat with him.

He went as far as stressing how he 'freely' had access to the Presidential villa. But, this was a man with a heavy burden of looking for a job for his son! He was begging people to assist him get a job for his son. Once, I had cause to ask him: "Since you're in close relationship with Mr President, why don't you meet him for a job for your son?" His answer was just f-u-n-n-y! He said: "Oh! I don't like discussing such issues with him. I know he can assist me, but I don't want that. I was even with him last night, and we had dinner together." What a fake person! As a matter of fact, the man came with a rickety taxi, and complained that his 'Jeep' was with the mechanic. You can imagine. If that type of person was living a decent and transparent lifestyle, he would have stood a chance of better opportunities because people would have offered him some assistance.

Let us strive to remove all the masks and pretentiousness in us, destroy all the stories, labels, and judgements that we have placed upon ourselves, so that our true selves will emerge. In as much as we should not allow ourselves to be deceived, we should, equally, not deceive others. Let us always be what and who we are.

Stop 'Acting'

Some people are busy with the question: "How will I act to get others to accept me?" Come off that, because, acting can expire but your true self is everlasting. You do not need to bend to fake expectations when you can easily be yourself. Follow your intuition. You might not always have your expectations met or be accepted but you will not need to have to keep up an act that you might forget. Reminds me of the story of a passenger who kept regaling his fellow passengers with one story to the other of one place he had visited to the other. At one of his pauses, one of the passengers remarked: "Sir, you know a lot of places and have travelled wide. You must know Geography very well." The other passenger replied:"Yes, yes, my friend. In fact, I was in Geography only last week." Of course, this provoked ridicule from fellow passengers! You see! So, being yourself and being honest saves you from ignorant lies and embarrassments.

When you are fully connected with your true nature, you are paving way for your real self to shine forth. As Bernard M. Baruch, an American financier, who was an adviser to different US Presidents, puts it: "Be who you are and say what you feel, because those who mind don't matter and those who matter don't mind." We do not expect everyone to think alike; bring out your thoughts, while the other person brings out his. That makes the world to move on.

Do not pose as someone else, because your personality will be at stake.

Impersonation can ruin you if you are not careful. This is because, behind every mask lies a deep-rooted fear to express oneself and reveal to others who one truly is. Deep down, the person feels empty and lonely. Pretending to be someone else makes you more alienated. Any relationship you enter into through this practice, can never be genuine, as they are merely shallow and empty. There will not be any sincere communication built around pretence. Stop wearing a mask. You are not a masquerade, you know.

You Are You

If you are who you are and truly appreciate your uniqueness, you will realise that no one can be better than you. This is the ticket for attracting all your life's ideal situations. Recognising your importance and your peculiarity is a worthy way to move forward in life, because you are God's own masterpiece. Just take it that you are original, and extremely valuable. Alex Gaskarth, singer and rhythm guitarist, advises thus: "Be real, because a mask only fools people on the outside. Pretending to be someone you're not takes a toll on the real you, and the real you is more important than anyone else."

You have an assignment, as you are full of gifts. Because you can leave a mark on this generation, be bold and stand on your identity. You can achieve this by loving yourself, creating a life you adore, rightly connecting to your passions/interests, self-care, obeying your intuition, committing to yourself, and your natural inclination. Believe truly in yourself. This demands your acceptance that you are who you are, and no one else. You can quickly agree with Dr. Seuss[12], the cartoonist, who stated: "Today, you are You, that is truer than true. There is no one alive who is 'Youer' than You."

Disadvantages Of Fake Life

Primarily, when you are not being yourself, your positive qualities cannot grow. This is because you will be busy, using all your energy in trying to accomplish what you want to project, losing energy you might have used in building your positive qualities. You will lose yourself in trying to become someone else.

Practising a fake life will waste a lot of your energy and time. Why? Because you will use much energy and time to come up with different ways to speak and do things when you are not being yourself. You know that if you are being yourself, what you say will come out naturally.

Being Yourself - Life Booster

You will always be at peace with yourself if you are not having a fake life. When you are at peace with yourself, your mind will be at rest because you will notice and enjoy the intricacies of your inner self. Consider a situation where you will not have anything to prove to anyone because, already, you are yourself. That means you are at your best. If, for instance, you did not tell someone a lie about being a relation to one influential character or the other, you are not expecting anyone to call you up to come and prove it. If you did not impersonate as a doctor, whereas you are a clerk, no one will expect you to come and defend or prove your identity.

When you are being yourself, you can inspire others. Millions of people who lack confidence worldwide can be inspired by your exemplary life. They will come to understand the need for them to be confident, and follow their heartbeats. You will gain higher level of respect when you are not living a fake life. People will admire your spirit, your courage, your confidence, and your level of honesty. The level of respect you will earn yourself knows no bounds because, you are already known by your true identity. You are someone that nobody can stop from what you are doing, because there is no fake display by you.

Many people live in fear and that is why some fake their identities. However, being yourself gives you the benefit of not living in fear. The choices you make in life are no longer dependent on what other people will think, whether you will be judged, disliked, or rejected. You will focus on being you. Due to the fact that being yourself makes you to have less stress, you will become more productive. When you reject living as who you are not, your productivity in your work, your play and your life in general will skyrocket.

Better decisions are made when you are being yourself. This is because they will be based on how you feel deep down, not based on your trying to copy someone. If you are able to make decisions by yourself, you will not have a complicated lifestyle. So, being yourself earns you this attribute. You are disposed to make better decisions when it is decision time. You cannot afford to copy someone else's decision. In your career, being yourself makes you take credit when your successes are as a result of your own original making. If you compare the work you have put your stamp on with those times when you have hidden your opinions and worked to the specifications of others, you will feel fulfilled. So, being yourself leads to you appreciating yourself more.

Being yourself keeps you happier. The happiest days of your life are as a result of doing the things you want to do (of course, the positive things), being the person you are meant to be, doing the things you believe in, and most importantly, being honest with yourself. You will be happier in life when you are simply yourself. Leo Tolstoy, the Russian novelist and moral philosopher, and who ranks as one of the world's great writers, says: "If you want to be happy, be." Being the person you are meant to be, makes you feel very happy. Do not forget that your happiness comes before anything else. When you like yourself, others will like you. People can always tell when others are not real. When you are in tune with yourself, those around you will get to know and like the real you as well.

Surely, confidence attracts confidence, so, being yourself for the sake of being yourself will attract more authentic people into your life, and create a network of supportive, uplifting, and even fun folks you can genuinely call friends. When people trust you because of your honesty, courage, confidence, you will really feel good. Naturally, people will not feel comfortable with anyone who cannot say a few words without telling a lie. After all, George MacDonald, Scottish author, poet and Christian minister observes that "to be trusted is a greater compliment than being loved." Only the right type of friends will be attracted to you, because they take you for who you truly are. As you engage in the business of your personal growth, doing what is natural to you, and staying true to your heart, you will always bring out your best. Relax, and be YOU.

~ Leave Me Alone ~

1. As I look at every angle
   I feel that I can dangle
   Since life is so glorious
   I just have to be joyous.

2. You may have your own pleasure
   And regard it as your treasure
   You may view it with compassion
   But don't joke with my passion.

3. Great joy for one to be oneself
   Why do you want to change yourself
   Why do you make yourself so fake?
   When you could live richer with
   nothing at stake?

4. If you stand on your right
   You will attain the height
   Be empowered by full clarity
   And you will get your liberty.

5. No matter the condition
   I have my own ambition
   You have your own to follow
   And not my own to swallow.

Chapter 11
Time Is Your Friend

Time is a measure in which events can be ordered from the past through the present into the future, and also the measure of duration of events and the intervals between them. It helps us structure our daily lives and activities so that we can live more organised and productive lives. We are all dependent on time. Time is applied in our every activity, from morning till night. Consequently, it is our companion and friend. We are all obliged to move with it, since it does not wait for anyone.

If you avail yourself to time, it will provide all its services to you. As long as there is time for everything, you can do everything within the time allotted to it. The proper management of time is required, for one's gift to empower him. It is the only thing that is impartial. It cannot cheat you.

There Is Time For Everything
Time is the most important commodity in our lives. It is needed for everything. There is time to be born and time to die; time to eat and time to rest; time to play and time to work, and so on. It cannot be stored, because everyone, no matter how rich or poor, spends it the same way. It cannot speed up for the rich or slow down for the poor. It never comes back.

Once the time for any calling comes up to you, you just have to obey. Your gift has a time to fully unfold, and no one can stop it. This is why we are always warned to do the right things at the right time, for them to be meaningful. You cannot expect a toddler, for instance to start riding a bicycle. It simply does not make sense because the time is not right for that. Time creates experience that enables one to accomplish certain tasks and feats.

Time Is Impartial
Everyone has the same number of hours, minutes, seconds, days, weeks, years. Why then should someone complain that he does not have enough time? It is simply because of abuse of time - mismanagement. Every activity takes time to accomplish. So, why the rush?

Albert Einstein, the most influential physicist, stated: "the only reason for time is so that everything doesn't happen at once." Even the Biblical quotation that, "to everything, there is season, and a time to every purpose under the heaven..."(Ecclesiastes 3:1) wonderfully captures the essence of time. In fact, time is the most precious thing in life; it influences every single moment and everything we do. Consequently, we need to value it.

Of great interest here is the quote by Leonardo Da Vinci, an Italian painter, sculptor, architect, musician, mathematician, engineer, inventor, anatomist, artist, geologist, cartographer, botanist, philosopher, and writer, widely considered to be one of the greatest painters of all time and perhaps, the most diversely talented person ever to have lived, and, who has often been revered as a man of 'unquenchable curiosity' and 'feverishly inventive imagination'. Among his works, the *Mona Lisa,* is the most famous portrait, while *The Last Supper* is regarded as the most reproduced religious printing of all time. Da Vinci, revered for his technological ingenuity, stated: "Time stays long enough for anyone who will use it." We can affirm that this is always available to use at our discretion, if only we can make it our friend. Time has no holiday, as it exists always, hence, our full disposition to make good use of it. Since it is a free force, it moves without any control, by anyone, and no one can ever get back the lost minute or second. You just have to strike the iron when it is hot. Time flies without returning, and if you waste it, it wastes you.

Time Heals Wounds

Time plays a great role in our lives. It is taken to be good medicine, because it heals wounds. You can imagine a situation whereby someone is bereaved. The pain continues to disturb the bereaved, but with time's aid, the pain of the loss disappears. The case of suffering from a particular sickness is another reason to see the goodness of time. With time and good treatment, the sickness is healed.

Jim Henson, an American puppeteer, an influential children's entertainer, best known for creating *The Muppet Show*, a US television series, has another admirable quote on time. His characters were a key component of *Sesame Street*, the children's educational television programme seen worldwide. According to Henson, "only time can heal your broken heart, just as only time can heal his broken arms and legs." Time gives you the opportunity to forget the past, forget the mistakes, and focus on what you are doing in your life today. The fact that you are able to unfold new opportunities, new breakthroughs, new achievements in life, is because time has been made available to you. The pain you were experiencing before has now been brushed aside by time. Your deep thoughts on those ugly experiences have begun to fade away, because of the passage of time. How great time is! "My pains are no more there!" – That is your new song.

Time Is A Reminder

The saying that experience is the best teacher, is attributed to time. The passage of time allows an individual to grow, and be reminded of certain important events. Since this enhances people's decision-taking ability, it can be considered as a counsellor, because it reminds one to act wisely. Because of time, we are able to make plans of action, thereby coming up with year planners, proposals, birthday celebrations, commemorations, and so on. Through these, we are constantly being reminded to act accordingly and promptly.

Complaining about lack of time makes you appear as if you are not part of nature. It only becomes imperative then that you plan wisely, because, there is time for everything to take its course. Since we know that time is powerful, and conquers all, we have no better choice than to make it our friend. Be a friend of time, so that you will not '*miss the train*'.

Manage Your Time Skilfully

For you to be a true friend of time, you need to manage it skilfully. You have to prioritise your actions and know which ones are urgent and which needs to be treated first. You may have up to four activities in a particular day, for instance: washing your clothes, going to the market, cooking food, and visiting a friend. Of course, the priority should not be visiting a friend, because, that may take the whole day, and that will make you complain later that you did not have enough time to finish washing your clothes.

Every task demands its own time. Even the washing machine in the house allots time to the quality/quantity of clothes you pack in there, for laundry services. Mere sleeping has its own time, so that you do not sleep from the night till 11:00am the following day, wasting the time you are supposed to use in going to work or to school, or conducting one business or the other.

Time Affords You Better Organisation

With proper time management, you will see yourself being more organised. Your thoughts will not be scattered, because, you have already allotted time to each activity and consequently, done a good planning. Each task will have enough time to materialise, and this will help you finish more jobs with less stress. Since we have limited time for every activity, the need to manage time cannot be overemphasised. It helps you make better decisions, and consequently, earns you more success in your endeavours. Time management creates discipline in you, as you are led to restrict your time to any ventured activity, rather than procrastinating. It equally makes you learn more.

The ability to learn more is a product of time management. Some students in the school indulge in truancy and other vicious activities throughout the period of studies, only for them to start 'burning the midnight oil' during exams. However, the wise ones start preparing for the exams right from the onset of the academic year, creating time to play, and time for serious studies. That is why you see well-prepared students going to sleep as early as 8:00 pm during exam period, because, they are ready for the examination.

Some people may wish to attend a particular occasion, scheduled to start by 10: 00am, only for them to set out of the house by 9:55 am. Such people end up rushing and speeding and start beating the traffic lights here and there, and even causing accidents on the roads. Time use, calls for caution. When we plan well and adhere strictly to the schedule, we notice that there is really no need to rush anything. The availability of time gives us opportunity for better organisation. To meet time, work towards setting early and reaching targets.

Waiting For Tomorrow?

Procrastination is said to be an enemy of time. Why postpone what you can comfortably do today till tomorrow? In essence, why leave till later what can be done now? You have the ample opportunity to improve your life today and start being creative, but you keep on postponing when you will unfold your talent. The language of 'till tomorrow' can never help you out, rather, it will compound your problems.

Time makes your bed, so you simply have to lie on it and enjoy it. Waiting for tomorrow means you are wasting so much of your life. Tomorrow might be late, maybe even too late. This is because you would not know what will happen in the next moment. Philip Stanhope, 4th Earl of Chesterfield, puts his thought on time thus: "Know the true value of time; snatch, seize, and enjoy every moment of it. No idleness, no laziness, and no procrastination: never put off till tomorrow what you can do today." Nothing, of course, is guaranteed in life, so you need to make good use of any available opportunity today.

People who wait for tomorrow to start living life and/or start improving on their lives fail to understand that tomorrow starts today. Try to do something today, to prepare for tomorrow. Remember that you will never get today back into your life, after it has gone.

This Is Your Opportunity

For the youths, this is your opportunity to make great use of your time. This is a period that one's life booms, and the best is unveiled. One inspirational quote on youths is from Kofi Anan, the Ghanaian diplomat, who served as the 7th Secretary General of the United Nations (from 1997 to December 2006). According to him, "Young people should be at the forefront of global change and innovation. Empowered, they can be key agents for development and peace. If, however, they are left on society's margins, all of us will be impoverished. Let us ensure that all young people have every opportunity to participate fully in the lives of their societies." He goes on further to say: "No one is born a good citizen; no nation is born a democracy. Rather, both are processes that continue to evolve over a lifetime. Young people must be included from birth. A society that cuts off from its youth severs its lifeline."

Young people are better when it comes to execution, rather than counsel. They are the ones to comfortably execute new projects. They are more disposed to inject new ideas into a system than older people. How do they perform when given the task or given opportunity in government? We cannot know their worth unless they are put to test – which is not often the case in Nigeria. Of course, the saying goes that 'the taste of the pudding is in the eating'. But maybe we should let time decide on when these young ones will also be given the chance to head.

The adults who are privileged to be in certain high ranking positions, how are you using the opportunity given to you? Remember that the clock ticks every time, indicating that time moves on and on without waiting for you to perform the required task from you. Time is related to history for the present quickly becomes the past and history. When you do nothing, time will judge you and woe betide you if the judgment passed is not favourable.

The fact that the work in various offices are somehow correlated, calls for caution on the use of our time. Most actions are dependent on previous actions. Why do you sit down on a file that needs to be treated, realising that the next officer cannot treat such file without your releasing it? Conscience should be a watchword in such circumstances. You have opportunity to rearrange your thoughts, and focus on positive touch towards humanity, using your opportunity. So, wherever you are, whatever you do, ensure that you let the job you are doing pass through so that the next person can move on. Time depends on you!

Time Is Not Your Enemy

To manage time is to manage life, so you need to play the game of time carefully. Some people complain that time is their enemy. This is because of the fact that they allow distractions to set in when they are about to achieve something: they do not use organiser, which helps them to plan their activities; they do not peg a time limit to each task; they do not set reminders; they do not focus on a particular key of each time; they do not delegate; they do not prioritise; they do not have a clock visibly placed before them; they do not create a daily plan.

You need to plan your day before it unfolds. This helps a great deal, so that you will not shout: "I ran out of time." When you follow the prescribed steps, you will definitely find out that time is your friend. Time is so faithful and strong that you cannot tame it, you only ride it; you cannot fight it, you can only follow it, for the friendship to be truly established. It is impartial, as it is always available to everyone. It has never disappointed anyone, since it does not change its way of operating. The way it functions on a Sunday is the same way it functions on a Friday. The same number of seconds make one minute each day, the same number of minutes make up one hour for all the days of the week, and the same number of hours make up each day. It is not, and can never be, your enemy.

~ **My Impartial Friend** ~

1. I call on you, dear Time
Come, come, walk with me
In you I see no crime
Much trust, I place in thee

2. You have your special measure
In our daily activities
For everyone to treasure
During all our festivities.

3. You are known to be impartial
Even with all your force
And you will never be partial
Right from your genuine source.

4. As we accord you right management
You reciprocate with reminders
Pulling us out from all banishment
And making us great providers.

5. Your ability to heal
Makes you to be highly cherished
You make our lives so real
That we get you established.

Chapter 12
Move With The Trend

Trends simply refer to a prevailing tendency or inclination at a particular time. It is a 'current' style. The ICT - Information and Communication Technology, which refers to all the technology used to handle telecommunications, broadcast media, intelligent building management systems, audio-visual processing and transmission systems, and network-based control and monitoring functions, is now a household name in Nigeria. That is the trend that most people are involved in, and they are using it towards their success. For us to fully embrace this concept, we all need to be taught valuable knowledge and skills around computing and communications devices, software that operates them, applications that run on them, and systems that are built with them. The knowledge of these will enhance productivity in all establishments - schools, offices, business settings, religious organisations, and so on. This translates to the ability of someone to commit to greater use of the talents he has.

Sometime ago, a man approached me in the office, while I was transferring files from one computer to the other. Surprised, he asked me: "Lady, so you know how to operate all these?" I looked at him and answered with a smile, "Why not?" He confessed that he had not really made out time to go into such "stressful" actions. I was quick to react: "Stressful?" Unfortunately, he had not yet understood that the essence of going into computer usage was to make my work less stressful. It is true that the beginning of anything is always tedious but the results are always worth it; the ends justify the means. I vividly remember that when I started learning how to use a computer, I felt stressed up, but I thank God for my computer instructor who was always patient with me. The reward for my determination and his patience? Today, I have joined one of the major trends: I am ICT compliant!

ICT - A Necessity
The truth is that computer literacy is a must for everyone if you wish to be comfortable in this century. What can you do these days without that? The

ultimate is to move with the trend of events. When others are joining Facebook, for instance, create your own page and use it, but wisely. When others are on Twitter, follow them to tweet. When others are sending mails via emails, sign up, and create your own email address. You are simply making your life to be smoother and much easier.

It was in the year 2000, under the Obasanjo administration, that Nigeria developed a policy on Information Technology (IT), with the aim of making Nigeria an IT adapted country in Africa. It was further aimed at making Nigeria a leading player in the use of ICT as an implement for sustainable development and global competitiveness[13]. This has changed the lot of the country for the better. Many people have keyed into this perspective. From indications on the way people are moving, the world may leave behind anyone that is not ICT compliant.

Easier Lifestyle

There is no doubt that the use of ICT has changed our lifestyles. You can visualise a lecturer delivering lectures through power presentations. The students are having access to better perceptions of what is being discussed through the slides used in these presentations. The lecture is even made more interesting and the students can take these presentations to study later.

Our daily financial transactions online (through online and mobile banking) are really giving a whole lot of people relief. One can sit in the comfort of one's home to send money to loved ones or conduct business transactions without going to the bank. One can also easily book flights without driving to the airport; send mails without going to the post office; chat with loved ones without travelling to their places of abode. How else could life be easier?

ICT – Playing Great Roles

ICT has an impact on almost all aspects of our lives. It has impact on our social lives, our learning methodology, and our working environment. The digital age has transformed the way young people communicate, network, seek help, access information, and learn.

The current young generation are now an online population, and access is through a variety of means, such as TV, computers, and mobile phones. People communicate via social media, such as: Skype, MySpace, 2go, WeChat, Badoo, Google+, Instagram, YouTube, Buddy, LinkedIn, Flickr, Pinterest, Twitter, WhatsApp, Facebook, and so on. Social media are computer-mediated tools that allow people to create, share, or exchange information, ideas, and pictures/videos in virtual communities and networks. It is defined as "a group of internet-based applications that build on the ideological and technological foundations of Web 2.0 and that allow the creation and exchange of user-generated content." It has been broadly defined to refer to "the many relatively inexpensive and widely accessible electronic tools that enable anyone to publish and access information, collaborate on a common effort, or build relationships."

The ICT is a great tool for change. We are all witnesses of the growing number of websites and help lines as forms of technically mediated service delivery. ICT has transformed career information and guidance services. Service delivery in other sectors such as banking and health services are equally transformed through this means.

In the school, ICT is a very necessary tool for the support of schools, in sharing experience and information with others, increasing a variety of educational services, promoting technology literacy, developing a system of collecting and disseminating educational information, implementing the principle of life-long learning and education.

Negative Influences

There is no doubt that, in anything that has advantages, you will find some disadvantages. Moving with the trend here implies moving with the positive trend, not the negative. The lives of students are highly influenced through the use of the open source tool - the internet. They are unfortunately prone to browsing the negative, such as pornographic sites and wasting their time on multimedia or online games. Eventually some get addicted, and devote just a little time to study, while some do not even wish to attend lessons.

These ugly practices, the school authorities can eradicate, by equipping the students with educational games. There are a lot of educational games which enhance the brain and have the capacity to make students more active in class. These are mathematical games, construction games, and the like. These will intellectually occupy their minds. The children can equally be motivated to have their own blogs on the internet, where they can be posting their articles, poems, news, and short stories. It will be an avenue for them to share their experiences through their own blogs. They can even create innovations in web design, which will be useful to their future.

Benefits

The use of ICT has many benefits. It has high speed delivery and wide reach, at low cost. In fact, there is instant delivery of information. Unlike in the olden days when it was taking a very long time to deliver information, with the use of ICT, most deliveries are instant. It does not matter where you are or how the weather is, you can always access and learn from ICT. When people access the same information across the world, there will be a uniformity of learning all over the globe.

ICT individualises learning, since it is not obligatory for the teacher to stand in front of the student before learning can take place. Each learner relates to the medium and its content. This equally reduces the cost of education. Rather than going to special centres to pay exorbitant fees for just a few hours, you can comfortably get educated through ICT, without paying so much. It can serve multiple teaching functions and diverse audiences, as they are used to diagnose and solve problems, access information and knowledge about various related themes. Officers and trainers get information through the vast available solutions to the questions that may have been posed. It is a reliable means of getting quick solutions to questions.

The importance of ICT in education cannot be overemphasised. Learners are motivated and purposely engaged in the learning process when concepts and skills are experienced with technology. And as technology becomes more and more embedded in our culture, we must provide our learners with relevant and contemporary experiences that allow them to successfully engage with technology and prepare them for life after school.

Most media operations were via analogue means, once upon a time. These days, the ultimate is to go digital. In broadcasting, for instance, most of the media houses are transforming from analogue to digital, to meet up with the demands of the jet age. One of the advantages of digital television is that it offers a growing range of fully interactive applications, allowing for interaction between viewer and broadcaster. It provides better picture and sound quality, improved flexibility of use, because of better portable and mobile reception, and a wider choice of programmes from a greater number of channels and radio stations.

Play Caution

I recognise the fact that some people are abusing the use of social media, but that is not a reason for you to dump it and regard it as childish affair. It depends on what you use it for. The people who introduced such have their aims but it is left for the user to use his wise discretion. You can equally send your message and advice through such. You can empower people to do the right thing through that medium too.

Parents and teachers are strictly advised to watch their wards. When you are aware of the societal issues, you will always be on guard for your children. They are your precious gold and silver, your jewels of inestimable value, so do not allow the wind of change blow them off from you. Be conscious and cautious. ICT remains the fastest, easiest, cheapest, and most accessible way of reaching your target audience. The only advice is that we should always be cautious. .

Moving With Other Trends

Apart from ICT, there are trends that abound that one should adopt, particularly if one wants to move ahead. Once upon a time, having a Degree was the ultimate. These days, it is only the starting point. To be successful in any profession, even business, it pays to have a Degree in at least one course. To become more effective and increase one's employment opportunities, one has to get a Master's Degree or pick special skills like ICT discussed at length above, adding foreign language skills or even getting a professional certificate from the abounding professional organisations like that of the Institute of Chartered Accountants of Nigeria (ICAN) or the National Institute of Management (NIM). These skills and the extra educational certificates enhance one's viability in the job market. More than that, the experience that leads to acquiring them increases one's knowledge. It helps you have more knowledge of the field in which you have studied.

Other trends of the moment include the entertainment sector. A lot of artistes are making a lot of money and acquiring fame due to their hard work. Lots of comedians and musicians have become household names as discussed at length in Chapter two. There are more opportunities open to the willing mind.

This chapter has sought to give an insight, touching only lightly on the various trends that one can key into if one is to be successful. As you do more research, you will find the one you can identify with. These days, there is no excuse as there is something for everyone. Follow what aspect of today's trend you feel can work for you.

~ Keep Moving ~

1. In this era of Facebook
You have a chance to showcase your outlook
But be wise to get a guidebook
That will give your life a greater look.

2. Your real romance with a computer
Will surely make you greater
It might be hard, but do not titter
Go on, learn, relearn, never be a quitter.

3. As the cursor obeys the mouse
So bricks of thoughts shall hold the
mental house
That will help espouse
Ways that will many life fires douse.

4. In a bid to edify
What we need to modify
We surely need to clarify
Things on which we shall surely testify.

5. There is a call to be bright...
If one would reach a greater height...
Forge on in the fight
Stand firm; you will find the light!

Chapter 13

Be Friendly

Being friendly is all about making people feel comfortable and loved, wherever you find yourself. It is a great means of paving way for the manifestation of your gift. Some people think it is a very difficult task, and so, do not co-operate with others. Some others are too proud to open up to other people, to share joy with them.

It costs relatively little to be friendly. Friendly environment makes you not to get heated up. As a matter of fact, it takes much more muscles for you to express your anger than your joy, so why go for the stress?

You Have To Be Approachable

For you to be friendly, you need to be approachable. Looking at some people's faces will scare you from getting close to them. They squeeze their faces. It is not a way to attract love from people around you. A little smile on your face does the magic. Go further to laugh easily, when you feel people need a boost of support or confidence.

When you ask people questions about themselves, you are already showing interest. That is the friendliness we are talking about. Show that you care. For instance: "How was the lecture today?" "How are your children doing at school?" "What television features do you like watching?" Questions of this kind are endearing and bring people together while creating a social air. Why don't you try it when next you find yourself around people, especially strangers?

Show Keen Interest

In a bid to make people feel your friendliness, try not to engage yourself in unnecessary distractions. During a conversation with someone, do not 'show off' by trying to punch on your iphone, ipad, and the like. It is also not nice to make unnecessary phone calls. It is rude and socially wrong. Drop all those distractions, for you to be able to show more friendliness. If need be, take excuse before you use any of your gadgets or make a call. It is not only polite but also shows respect.

A Little Compliment As Morale Booster

Some people never compliment others for their good deeds, and this is really discouraging. Good deeds deserve compliments. So also does the physical disposition of the person close to you. This helps to make the relationship flow more smoothly. What is wrong in saying: "I like your hair do," "Your handbag is really pretty and nice," "You are a bright student," "I like your method of teaching," "Your programme on the radio is superb," "I think you are a fantastic writer" and so on? Such compliments move the person to perform more. There is an old adage that says: "when you praise someone for what he has done, he will do yet another one." If you do not readily see what to compliment, just pause and think of one awesome quality the person has that appeals to you. It is important to only pass honest compliments. Anything else will be false and can dent your image… So, be careful.

Your Body Language Matters

Mastering of open body language will move you into friendlier atmosphere. You will not expect someone to come close to you when you cross your legs, cross your arms, lean backward, or maybe, stand with arms akimbo. Try to lean forward toward other people, have a good posture, keep your legs together, and be always ready to offer a handshake.

Your eye contact matters a lot, for a friendly environment. This makes people around you realise that you care and that they are not really wasting your time. Staring on the floor when you are supposed to be fully engaged in a conversation with someone, can put that person off. The more people see the beauty in your eyes and looks, the more they are attracted to you. Some may even feel 'you are hiding some cockroaches in the cupboard', by removing your eyes from them.

Get Closer

Do you wonder why some people insist on knowing your names? It is simply to get closer to you. By using your names when you are conversing with people, you feel some kind of closeness between you and the people with whom you are conversing. You can easily differentiate the expression, "How is the weather treating you today?" from "Uche, how is the weather treating you today?" I feel the second one sounds friendlier. What do you think?

Not only does it create a friendlier environment. It also makes the people conversing distinguish themselves as individuals, and they will be happy to note that. Surprisingly, some people live together without freely calling others by their names! They simply draw close to them and deliver the message they wish to convey. This practice is not encouraging at all. You should call the real names or pet names you wish to use. That's being friendly.

Being friendly, does not, in any way, mean being fake. You just need to show genuine interest in people, as it is one of the keys to being a friendly person. For you to be actually called a friendly person, you need to be concerned about the psychological dispositions of people around you, knowing when they are upset or happy. Some people take delight in seeing others feeling unhappy. Such people even go to the extent of talking to people to become cooler. What will you gain from such a practice? Practically, nothing positive.

Upholding self-confidence and overcoming your insecurities will open you up to be a friendlier person. Rather than confining yourself to your bedroom or corner, due to fear of unacceptability and distrust, leaving yourself to rot away, without gathering people around to make your life more cherishing, feel courageous to walk into people, not minding about what you think of yourself, and establish a relationship.

Check Your Social Life

How is your social life? This is a genuine issue to consider, if one wants to work on being a friendly person. You need a bustling social life if you want to be more friendly. You need to get used to meeting people and talking to them. Your social engagements should be richer. As a matter of fact, if you don't attend social engagements like weddings and birthday parties, for instance, how will you be able to organise your own when you ought to? Many other activities exist, which can take you out on a social spree – swimming, cycling, football, and so on. Your work or other commitments should not fully deprive you of other social engagements, because, you equally need them, to balance your lifestyle.

Have you ever tried to initiate a talk with a new person? This demands caution, anyway. When you have studied the disposition of that person, go on and initiate a conversation. That is a way of being friendly to a stranger. The stranger may be a new neighbour, a new class mate, someone sitting next to you in a party, in a taxi cab, in a plane, and so on.

Being a friendly person demands that you focus on positive topics during conversation. Rather than keep on complaining about power failure, lack of good roads, hike in prices of goods, and all those negative issues, try to uphold topics that will uplift the mind and give you awesome and relaxed moments.

What about that interesting TV show you watched? How about that child that knows how to show acrobatic displays in the school? What about that delicious meal that makes you feel real good? Put more fun into your conversations.

Avoid Cold Shoulder

There's nothing as nasty and embarrassing as giving someone a cold shoulder! Someone may pleasantly be greeting you, only for you to simply say 'hi', and continue walking! Consider yourself being treated like that. As a human being, you are bound to have people who are less advantaged than you, and, of course, some others who are greater than you. Politeness and humility pave way for you in this case. Do unto others what you wish them to do unto you. That is the golden rule.

Give Out Invitations

You can open up room for more friends through invitations. To be friendly means that you need to spend some more time with other people. You can give out invitations to people for a birthday, a little concert show, or even a house get-together. Just be brave to do that, and you will be surprised at the type of response you will get. Through that means, people can get to know more of other people through introductions by you. That makes life to go on more smoothly and pleasantly.

Apart from inviting people, you should equally be ready to accept more invitations from people. That is a great way of making you friendlier. Some people are so glued to their work or business that they find it difficult to say "yes" to an invitation. How do you expect to grow when you cannot even honour other people's invitations? That is the difference between a human being and an animal. An animal can never meet another animal to scratch its back; rather, it will scratch it on a tree or a wall. But, a human being will simply ask a fellow human being to scratch his back. Too much excuse will not solve problems when it comes to real human intimate relationships. Prove your worth by making yourself available to the person who invites you. You're simply showing friendliness.

Show Love

You have to show love, which is the greatest virtue. Nobel laureate, Bertrand Russel, a British philosopher, logician, historian, mathematician, educationist, social critic, essayist, and political activist, had this to say: "The secret of happiness is this: let your interests be as wide as possible, and let your reactions to the things and persons that interest you be as far as possible friendly rather than hostile."

Being friendly cannot be restricted to any particular group of people. If, for example, you are a boss in the office, nothing stops you from chatting with workers when they are not too busy. It does not reduce your personality in any way. As long as you humble yourself doing that, the response you will get from them is a standing ovation. If you are in business, your friendly disposition will naturally attract more customers to you. I remember one woman whose goods would always be exhausted before her fellow market women would sell theirs. This is because of her friendly strategy towards all who come in contact with her.

More Open Doors For You

Being friendly attracts open doors for you. A friendly person can never be stranded, because at every point in time, he will see people who will be of assistance to him. The most successful people in life are those who are friendly and kind. Their courteous nature attracts people to them rather than dispel them. If you are a friendly person, you will, naturally, have a lot of friends. You can never be alone, as a matter of fact. Loneliness is a disaster of its own, because it has many disastrous impacts on our lives. So, with many friends at your door, you will never experience a solitary life. Your life will always be a busy one.

Being friendly is rewarding, because, you will be more relaxed. You will not pay attention to all the little annoying things around you, as your friendliness gives you opportunity to enjoy life at its fullest. In fact, it improves your mental health greatly. You will bother yourself less, as you will be striving to see mainly the good aspects of life of someone to comment on. There is no doubt that one earns respect to one's self as a result of being friendly. People will surely appreciate your kindness, and that, consequently, will boost your self-respect. Nobody around you will like to pull you down because of the friendly way you have been dealing with them.

It is really good to be friendly, because it keeps you in the know. People will always spot you out for that needed encouragement, smile or fun. You too, can equally get unexpected benefits, especially at your trying moments. A friendly person always feels good about himself. This is because he will always be experiencing a feeling of fulfilment that he is actually nice to someone. Whenever I do good things to people, my inner self will always be having a positive vibration that some productive experiences are going on in my heart. In fact, I experience a feeling of satisfaction when I show friendliness to people.

Richard Stallman, a software freedom activist and computer

programmer, the most forceful and famous practitioner/theorist of free software, says: "Anything that prevents you from being friendly, a good neighbour, is a terror tactic." A friendly environment, devoid of tension, is what we need in our families, our offices, our schools, our markets, our business areas, and the like, because, that brings out the best in everyone. With that, we are assured of a very healthy and successful future.

People are more productive when they find themselves in friendly environments. A boss who is always shouting at his subordinates can never have much production, because of lack of co-operation from the staff. Brains respond positively to kindness, of course. One of the pills to swallow, during impatience, is being friendly. It is good therapy for running away from the intricacies of lack of patience. This attribute gives you opportunity to exercise your ability to be patient. Someone who may appear impolite or the like may come your way, but, making use of your friendliness will simply make the person bow for you.

~ **It Costs You Nothing** ~

1. *Becoming friendly*
Saves you from things that are deadly...
Put laughter and shy away from moaning
This will save you from mourning.

2. *What do you gain by frowning*
When you can begin smiling
And pose in healthy meekness
To have the desired closeness.

3. *Working on the expectation*
Results in huge consolation
Through your own commitment
You'll get the achievement

4. *Having all emotions endured*
Add smiles, for sweet life to be assured
Devoid of any tension
It brings a beauty to change any malfunction.

5. *Living in friendliness*
Will yield you much cleanliness
And you will be so comfortable
That your life becomes really honourable.

Chapter 14
Don't Be A Victim Of Intimidation

Nobody can make you feel inferior without your consent – Eleanor Roosevelt

Intimidation implies the use of violence or threats to influence the conduct, or compel the consent of another. The victim is frightened or threatened, and usually persuaded to do something that may not be his wish. Rather than express one's self, one may find himself in a timid situation, prone to easy destruction, by someone else. This should not be your best disposition, because, you have every opportunity to be what you wish to be. It is you, and you alone, that can allow others to intimidate you, because you are the one to create room for that. You are the owner of yourself. Lack of self-confidence, courage, or bravery can lead someone to his doom.

Some people are easily frightened when it comes to taking decisions and making contributions. Such people are usually introverts. They would prefer not to be heard, to being criticised. "Don't be intimidated by the impossibility, be motivated by the possibility," so says Jim Craig on Twitter. Craig was best known as goalie for 1980 USA 'Miracle on Ice' Hockey Team). Intimidation traits are serious setbacks in the pathway of unlocking one's potential, so, they should be avoided by all means.

Fear & Lack Of Self-confidence
These are easily manifested when someone is intimidated. It is the fear of being bullied in the school, for instance, that will make a child feel intimidated about going back to the class. It is the fear of losing a job that will make an employee allow herself to be molested by her boss.

When you lack self-confidence, you cannot stand on your own. That is why you can be easily intimidated. The socio-psychological concept of self-confidence relates to self-assurance in one's personal judgement, ability, and power. Confidence is a tool you can use in your daily life. You use it to manage your fears, and become able to do more of the things that really matter to you. Being confident is not an end that you reach and then stop. You have to keep playing to the best of your ability, and your confidence will always be there to support you. Seeing progress gives you self-reinforcement. Rumi, a 13th century Persian poet, regarded as one of the greatest spiritual masters and poetical intellects, was one of the world's most revered mystical poets. He once stated that one should chart one's course. In his words, "Don't be satisfied with stories, how things have gone with others. Unfold your own myth."

Fear is a powerful enemy, and it can come in all shapes and sizes. It may be as a result of bad experiences we had in the past, or simply fear of the unknown future, or fear of failure, fear of public speaking, but, whatever your fears may be, they can stop you in your tracks. This can easily lead you to be a victim of intimidation. Try to be bold, because there is magic in boldness. You will use it to conquer social anxiety. The greatest challenge with fear is that it can hold us back from achieving our goals, but it does not have to. We need courage in times of fear, to surmount it.

Cases Of Intimidation

In the school systems, it is common to hear cases of students being intimidated by others. Some are intimidated by fear of bully by some senior students. This practice is witnessed in schools where the authorities may not be fully aware of what the junior students are suffering in the hands of the senior ones. Even when the authorities take action, the senior ones may still intimidate the younger ones with further threats.

As a Vice Principal in charge of Administration in one of the senior boarding secondary schools, I was opportune to witness and handle some of these ugly experiences the junior ones used to have. They were quite pathetic, because, some came into the boarding school at a tender age. Any conscientious administrator would never love to give chances to those bullies. The practice was that the senior boys used to wait for the junior ones to come back from night prep, for them to start 'pouncing' on them, with their belts, forcing them to kneel down, ordering them to go and fetch water for them, breaking their lockers to collect their provisions, and so on. In some cases where the senior students decided to go and fetch water, they would never allow any junior student to fetch until they were fully satisfied. Even when they fetched, they would order the junior ones to carry the water to the hostel for them.

That was a bitter pill for the junior boys then. However, the school management at that time, waved into the situation and acted in a responsive manner, to rescue those young boys. Many stringent measures were taken, to curb the practice, to the extent of making the senior boys realise that the ugly practice would lead them to their doom. When we made the stubborn ones understand that 'iron must bend', they came to terms with the reality of life: 'Do unto others as you want them to do unto you'. Today, most of those students have confessed that the discipline instilled in them then helped them to be better products of the school system and indeed, better people.

There are equally incidences of girls being intimidated because of their refusal of 'friendship' advances by the male students or male teachers. When that situation arises, the poor girls will be faced with the music of constant harassment, embarrassment, and failures in the school. In some cases, it is the teachers that are being intimidated by the affluent parents of some students. They are threatened to the point that some parents would never want to hear that their children are punished in the school for offences, which, definitely, they have committed. Their children are then regarded as 'sacred cows' by these poor teachers. In such cases, how do you expect productivity from that school, since the teachers in whom those children are entrusted, cannot take disciplinary measures against them? This question needs an objective response.

How about the intimidation of lecturers by students, causing them to fear their jobs and fear going out in public? Those high school teachers are intimidated by some occult students and even some of their parents when they are not satisfied with a grade, or when the need for discipline arises. Of equal note is the workplace intimidation. This is the practice of a repetitious mistreatment of someone, which can cause that person some major health, emotional, and psychological problems. Some of these intimidating behaviours include: verbally abusing you by yelling and screaming, putting you down and ridiculing you in front of others, along with sabotaging or stealing credit for your work. It can equally be characterised by offensive non-verbal actions, like creating circumstances that limit your ability to do your job. There are other instances of intimidation found in everyday life, like in the hospitals, parks, banks, houses, and in the streets.

Feel Free

When you feel timid, you are underrating yourself. Others will easily climb on you and even frighten you. That is why, in the school system, extroverts can never be intimidated, especially when it comes to various club activities. They are everywhere. Associate with others as if there is no threat to your life.

Regrettably, some people are agents of intimidation, just looking for someone to frighten, in order to get what they want. Beware of such people, and stand on your feet against such odds. You can equally intimidate such threatening people with your uniqueness, and they will bow for you. There are certain striking qualities like academic prowess, humility, high skill acquisition, honesty, and the like, you may have, which those agents of intimidation may not possess, so use that quality to 'knock' them down. Always shoot back with what you have, in a positive way, to flee from being intimidated.

Fight Back

I see situations where some illiterate rich people try to intimidate the poor ones near them, by boasting of their wealth and their ability to use money to call everyone to order. But, unfortunately for them, those poor but intelligent ones are equipped with academic power and technicalities. They are pushed to use 'big grammar' to pursue the rich but illiterate ones, from very important events. Do not allow circumstances to swallow you up. You are the engineer of your destiny, so construct the bridge in such a way that you can easily cross it.

In the film industry in Nigeria, we witness the success story of the popular actors, Chinedu Ikedieze and Osita Iheme[14], who have vowed never to be intimidated on the basis of their heights. Rather, they have used that as God's given uniqueness in them, to attract fans. As smallish as they may appear on the screen, they have created a commanding appearance that has attracted high admiration from fans across the world. Instead of adjusting to discuss with people who are much taller than they are, they 'command' others to 'reduce' their heights, to be on the same level with them, for discussions! Apart from taking the centre stage, they are adored on the streets, at events, at airports, and other related places. They are treated with respect everywhere they visit, because they have succeeded in putting smiles on people's faces during relaxation times. Today, they are heroes, and no one dares intimidate them. Get it?

We have to mould our talents to work for us without letting anyone make us feel belittled due to any challenge we might have, physically, socially, economically or in any respect.

Do Not Become Your Own Worst Enemy

The only person who should have influence on our self-worth is the one we see in the mirror everyday. Do not become your own worst enemy. Instead, become your own best advocate. If you come to terms with the fact that nothing in life is constant, you will appreciate the fact that there is neither absolute happiness nor absolute sadness. When you expect only contentment, then you are looking for trouble for yourself, because, life is such that humans must know misery to identify times of elation. You have to accept reality instead of fighting it. Sometimes, you let what you expected to happen blindfold you from all the good things that are happening around you. Just drop the needless expectations, hope for the best, but expect less.

Do not limit your beliefs in your capability. Since you are the one who controls your thoughts, the only person who can hold you down is you. Eleanor Roosevelt's quote reminds us of this: "No one can make you feel inferior, except yourself." Try to do what you think you cannot do, and you will be surprised to see that you can actually do it. Step out of your comfort zone and make more exploits. People are reluctant to pursue growth because they already feel complacent with their situations. That is simply not living, but mere existing, because living is about learning and growing through excitement and discomfort.

Another way you become your own worst enemy is through obsession with examining personal failures. This is to say that you are busy recounting what has not worked in the past. This is detrimental to your growth. You should channel your thinking to the positive influences in your life. That is the most efficient way to enjoy more successes in life.

Changing Your Thought Pattern

You can control intimidation through the ways you think, especially, about yourself. Through some negative self-talks, some people initiate intimidation into their minds. For instance, certain people might have such thoughts as "How can I face such a crowd?" "I don't think I can compete with that student", and so on. Stop thinking that things will go negatively with you. Rather, be positive in your thoughts.

Stop avoiding situations where you become intimidated, by so doing, you cannot easily overcome that fear. It is when you take the bold step of facing the music, with deep breathing, that you will have defeated intimidation. Do not think of how others will feel about you or your actions. Hold the power to your side and believe that you are the one holding the cards, not those around you.

Coming Out, Victorious

You deserve to stand strongly amongst even your greatest idols, 'superiors', and authority figures. When you consider certain judgements you will make by yourself, you will come to realise that you do not have to be a victim of intimidation.

When you disallow intimidation in your life, you can freely and easily integrate into strange situations. You will find it graceful to adapt to any new environment, after all, there is the popular saying that, "when you are in Rome, you behave like the Romans." Truly, I experienced it when I travelled to Rome (in Italy). I did not have any knowledge of Italian language or Latin, as to 'qualify' me to follow others to worship at the famous St Peter's Basilica, Rome, but I paved way for myself to partake in the worship. It was true that I did not understand the language, but I still had that devotion and communication with God inside there, without allowing anybody to intimidate or harass me.

If you understand your own worth, then, accept yourself, accept your history, accept the flaws you cannot change, and grow in all the ways you can. The people who intimidate you are not worth more than you. If you start thinking that people you meet may not love you or like you, it is likely this will be the case. They may even hurt you, as you might have thought, but believe in the good in you, and others will see it.

Acknowledge your ego. You are somebody! Do not have a feeling that you are less than someone else you look up to. Clean all the feelings of shyness, anxiety, nervousness, and low self-esteem, if you wish to plant yourself on the path of victory. Of course, as Joel Osteen, a popular motivational speaker, said "You cannot expect victory and plan for defeat."

Just be reminded that the person intimidating you is human, with his own challenges, family issues, societal expectations, insurmounted obstacles, and so on. They are not better than you in any way. They are simply not different from you. With these thoughts in mind, you will overcome that negativity in you.

~ Lost In The Crowd ~

1. If only you have the mastery
To run away from misery
And never to be swallowed
But rather to be followed.

2. Seeing the river overflowing
I cannot see you moving
How can you leave your name
And find someone else to blame?

3. You are moved to the right
You follow without might
They take you to the left
You move on like a guest.

4. It takes bravery
To bring one out of slavery
Rather than be intimidated or to intimidate
Focus on you and make yourself great

5. A life devoid of sorrow
Will never spoil your morrow
It gives you all the power
To reach that mighty tower.

Chapter 15
Be A Role Model

S imply put, a role model is a person whose behaviour, example, or success, is, or can be, emulated by others, especially by younger people. True role models are those who possess the qualities that we would like to have, and those who have affected us in a way that makes us want to be better people. A role model is the one being looked up to, and revered by someone else. An individual aspires to be like that person, either in the present or in the future. Through role models, one can unlock the potentials in him. Equally, by being a role model, one will perform excellently in such a way that his own potential will be fully unlocked.

Sometimes, we do not recognise people we are emulating until we have noticed our own personal growth and progress that they have caused. Your role model may be someone you know and interact with, or may be someone you have never met, such as a celebrity. Common role models include: well-known actors, public figures such as: administrators or political officials, teachers, or other educators, and parents or other family members. Definitely, a role model is admired by the one who wishes to be like he/she is. Through role models, individuals are able to unfold what is caged in them, as they often aspire to behave like such people.

The Child's First Contact

Before a child starts attending school, his first contacts are the parents. Therefore, the first role model of a child is the parent. Children are known for 'imitation', because they are not born with any social knowledge or social skills. Consequently, they follow the examples laid down by their parents. It is therefore pertinent that parents impact positively on the children.

By the time a child enters the school system, he is more exposed, and he starts identifying how some people are behaving in the society. Sometimes, through the media, something may make a child wish to be like a particular person. What really makes a child to shout "Oh! I want to be like Mr. A"? It is the *modus operandi* of Mr. 'A'. The child may see how active that person is in the society, how the person has touched lives, how the person uses his ability in cherished manners, the leadership quality of the person, his moral disposition, his intellectual aspect, and so on. But, in all, something in that person will definitely strike someone else to make him his role model.

Any Need For Role Model?

Is there really need for one to have a role model? You may ask. Of course, yes, because, honestly speaking it takes much courage and self-confidence to chart your own path. Role models are the ones who can define our course of action and the qualities that are required to attain those heights. Your role model can be your parent, your friend, your boss in the office, or any public figure. Role models assist you to succeed in life. They are the tape with which you rule yourself to see how much you have achieved.

A role model teaches someone that there is no shortcut to success, that hard work is the only key to that. A role model relays to you, the ability to stay focused in the face of failures and constant discouragement that comes along with it. Having a role model easily qualifies you to be a successful entrepreneur, as you will be led to follow him relentlessly.

Who Is Your Role Model?

Each person has a role model in his or her life. The role model could be a friend, a teacher, a neighbour, a father, a mother, a grand-parent, a sports hero, an actress, a newscaster, a doctor in your hospital, and so on. Your role model can be an ordinary person or a celebrity.

I can never forget the closeness between my mother and myself, and that is why she remains my role model. When I was young, I used to imitate the way she talked, joked, danced, taught, and encouraged people. She was a very sociable woman and an ingenious administrator. We saw in her, a model wife, a trustworthy friend, a caring mother, and a successful administrator in the school system. I kept on hoping to be like her. Honestly, I remain ever grateful to her for the inspiration I got from her. So, who is your own role model?

Everyone Should Be A Role Model

Barry Bonds, an American, and one of the greatest baseball players of all time says: "Everyone in society should be a role model, not only for their own self-respect, but for respect from others." When each person turns out to be a role model, people would rather concentrate on building themselves up, rather than waiting for others to dictate the pace for them.

When you aspire to be a role model, you will feel a special burden to perform well; you will always try to bring out good attributes that people will copy. Of course, you can never fight in the public, you will guard your mouth against negative utterances, you will always be mindful of the consequences of any action you wish to take, bearing in mind that your admirers are watching. When each person performs well, the society will be a better place for the growing populace.

Choosing A Role Model
Since role models help us become what we want to be, and inspire us to make a difference, you need to choose wisely. You can choose a role model in your personal life, and/or a celebrity role model. One can take personal life role models who one can mould one's life after. One can also take a professional life role model that one will model one's career after.

For your personal life, it is advisable to choose a role model that you know, because the person will help you mature and grow as a person, through guidance and advice, to achieve your best. You need to identify the people who exhibit the same qualities you wish to achieve. They may exist around you, and they have a more profound impact on you. Since the purpose of having a role model is to improve yourself, it is better to choose someone who makes you feel positive about yourself. You should identify the traits you want to change in you. These negative aspects of your personality will be focused on, when you want to choose a role model for yourself.

You need to find out people who have done something you admire in life. This may include great philanthropists who have given scholarship opportunities to students, some who have saved lives, some who have raised a lot of money for charity, and so on. Check for people who have reliable competence, and who have gained their positions through dedication and hard work. They are the most skilled. It is advisable to learn about the successes and failures of those you wish to emulate, because, the knowledge about their failures will encourage you to move from failure to success. You will realise that, they, like you, are only human, and can make mistakes.

For one's professional career, one needs to take a model related to one's field of choice. It only makes sense that if you want to be a writer, you should model your life after someone like Chinua Achebe, Wole Soyinka, Eugenia Abu, Hyginus Ekwuazi or any writer of note who has achieved great successes. For music, you can think of what music you want to indulge in, whether modern or classic, blues or reggae. This will determine whether you want to have Whiz Kid, Banky W, R. Kelly, Celine Dion, Mozart or Beethoven, as your choice model. You can either take a known person (a celebrity) or anyone around you who is dedicated to the profession you desire and has achieved some measures of success.

In choosing a celebrity role model, you need to play extra caution, because you learn about this person through the media rather than through personal observation. He is the hero who excels in a particular area you wish to emulate. Identify the person that is living life the way you would like to. If you want to be an actress, a musician, an author, or the like, then identify the ones whose worth you have clarified. It is important to also learn about their personal faults. For the celebrities, some of their personal lives may not be the ideal type for you, so you do not need to emulate all. After all, you equally have your own strengths.

You do not need to copy your role model completely, because, everyone makes mistakes. Your role models are simply there as a guide for you, so, you do not need to follow them blindly. Develop your own style because it is important to retain your personality. Above all, always stand out to make the best decision for yourself. It is your life and you have to live it.

Are You A Role Model?

At this point, it is pertinent to ask yourself the question: "Am I a role model?" Whether you choose to be or not, you are a role model to someone - maybe your child or your neighbour, or your student, or even your friend. So, you have a special task to perform well, for that person to be inspired. Rosa Parks, an African-American civil rights activist, whom the United States Congress called 'the first lady of civil rights', and 'the mother of the freedom movement', said: "Each person must live their life as a model for others." You have to be a reflection of your true self. Be practical about your status of being a role model.

How is your disposition affecting others? Is it positive or negative? But watch it. You are directly or indirectly changing someone's character. For the society to grow, the changes you are making in someone else should be positive. As a parent, you should teach your children how to make prayer their key to success. As a teacher, you should be handling the students in such a way that they will always wish to be like you. As a Chief Executive, you should not oppress your subordinates, thinking that they can never climb to that height. As a subordinate, you should not be a saboteur, forgetting that you will climb to the top someday. Everyone has a stake in the business of being a role model.

If you wish to be a good role model, you should think aloud, to allow the children see how you work through issues. Show them the best decision and help them arrive at the conclusion. Make positive choices so that the people who are looking unto you will note the exemplary lifestyle you are living, for them to follow such when they find themselves in critical conditions. When you make mistakes, you have to apologise, and let those around you know you made a mistake, and how you plan to fix such. This is because you are human, and not perfect.

You have to be well-rounded. You can be a parent and equally be a teacher, a musician, and a valuable friend in whom the child will trust. As for the parent, Lawrence Balter, a published author of children's books, advises: "The best way to teach a child restraint and generosity is to be a model of those qualities yourself. If your child sees that you want a particular item but restrain from buying it, either because it is not practical or because you cannot afford it, he will begin to understand restraint. Likewise, if you donate books or clothing to charity, take him with you to distribute the items, to teach him about generosity." This is more of practical than theoretical.

For you to be a good role model, you need to demonstrate confidence, so that others who wish to copy from you will be convinced of the path they wish to follow. The others who are looking unto you as their super heroes are looking unto you to show respect. If you take other people for granted, or refuse to show gratitude to others, you are not showing them the way to succeed. Be yourself, feel confident, stand out, and do the right, so that others will emulate you. Be a role model yourself.

~ I Like To Be Like You ~

1. Oh! What a passion you possess
That truly moves me to confess
That you are one in a million
Sitting right there in a pavilion.

2. I wish I could follow the rule
And never ever play the fool
In this my little ambition
To be like you with passion.

3. With all your traits so uncommon
You love those that are so common
Too difficult to get enraged
I'll never be discouraged.

4. That opportunity to display
The innermost feeling today
Moves me to come to you
Seeking earnestly to be like you.

5. How great you are in all your work
That's why I will cherish your worth
You move yourself with dignity
With every sense of sanity.

Chapter 16
Make Humility Your Watchword

There is nothing noble in being superior to your fellow man; true nobility is being superior to your former self – Ernest Hemingway

The word 'humility' signifies lowliness or submissiveness. It is that by which a man has a modest estimate of his own worth and submits himself to others. It is the quality or state of not thinking that you are better than other people. When this attribute is possessed by someone, the person will be in a more comfortable terrain to excel, thereby making his natural attribute a source of his power. Humility is a worthy virtue to be maintained and one I admire so much.

There is little or no gain from being proud. Realising that God who created you can change your condition at any time will make you always bow. So, do not feel superior to other human beings created by God. It is in the light of this that Ernest Hemingway, one of the most famous and influential American writers of the 20th Century states that "Humility is not disgraceful, and carries no loss of true pride."[15] Good talk.

Equally of relevance is the saying that, "on the highest throne in the world, we still sit only on our own bottom," as affirmed by Michel de Montaigne, a French philosopher, famously regarded as the 'Father of Modern Skepticism'. Montaigne showed great impact on the writers worldwide. He was an influential and key figure of the French Renaissance. He is best known for his essays which are considered to be the best of all times. His huge volume of essays, *Essais*, is still considered to be the finest collection of essays which influenced many other notable writers, such as René Descartes, Isaac Asimov, and William Shakespeare.

The earlier we accept that it is only through humility that we shall realise our worth, the better for us, in order to be realistic about life. Even if one has a mighty mansion, he needs to acknowledge the raw fact that he can only sleep in one room at a time. Inside that room, he can only lie on one bed at a time. On that bed, he can only occupy one side of the bed at a time! It is therefore pertinent that we succumb to the realities of life, so that we can come to terms with the potentials in us.

Pride Goes Before A Fall

This means that, if you are too proud and over-confident, you will make mistakes leading to your defeat. If you allow yourself get too proud, you will find yourself humiliated. Jesse Jackson,[16] the American civil rights activist, and one of the fiercest and outspoken political figures in the USA, warns thus: "Never look down on somebody unless you're helping him up." The problem with some people is that they are too proud to associate with others. They feel that it is too degrading mingling with other people who may not have had same opportunity of greatness with them.

Nobody is sure of tomorrow. Those people you are rejecting today may eventually be the ones that will save you in future. You should be nice to people on your way up because you'll meet them on your way down. This is a popular saying, and it needs to open our eyes, if we wish to achieve success in life. Nobody is an island. If you make yourself an island, no one can approach you or even make suggestions to you, as you will definitely reject all. "Humility is to make a right estimate of one's self," as Charles Haddon Spurgeon affirms. Spurgeon was British best-known Baptist minister. By the age of twenty-one, he was the most popular preacher in London. He remains highly influential among Christians of various denominations among whom he is known as the 'Prince of preachers'. People are positively touched by his teachings.

The case of a man who did not realise he was wearing his shirt the wrong way, is testing ground for smooth relationship with others. The fact that nobody could talk to him made the people who saw him dressed badly not to point it out for him. Incidentally, the man was going to serve as the Chairman of an occasion. He got the embarrassment of his life when the Master of Ceremony picked the microphone and funnily remarked that the chairman of the occasion dressed like one poor man in his village who used to alternate his dressing mode from front to back whenever he noticed that one side was dirty. It was only then that this proud and arrogant Chairman noticed that he dressed wrongly. That gave him the shame of his lifetime, because, everyone laughed at him in such a way that he quickly excused himself to go and 'ease himself'. From there, he never went back to the occasion. It was thenceforth that he started making consultations, without limitations, in all his actions. He was surely humbled.

Equally, Mr. Geoffrey, a business tycoon, who felt he had succeeded in life, attended an occasion, and, rather than wait to be called up to the high table, walked straight to that place. Unfortunately, he was called out from where he was seated, and was duly informed that the place was reserved for another person. Because he could not humble himself, he stumbled out of the hall, disgraced.

You Will Be Exalted

From the religious point of view, "Whoever exalts himself shall be humbled, and whoever humbles himself shall be exalted" (Mathew 23:12). A man, who humbly goes down to sit with others, even when he knows that his social status does not accommodate that, will surely be located. Of course, "a golden fish has no hiding place." According to William Temple, an American statesman and essayist, who successfully negotiated the marriage of William, Prince of Orange, and Princess Mary of England, "Humility does not mean thinking less of yourself than of other people, nor does it mean having a low opinion of your own gifts. It means freedom from thinking about yourself at all."

Sometimes, people try to force their ways through, but that does not solve any problem. The result is always provocative, as such people feel 'wounded' when they do not get what they want. Allow things to flow naturally. '*Que sera, sera*' (Whatever will be, will be), a popular song written by the Jay Livingston and Ray Evans song-writing team, brings us close to this reality. It is not really by making noise that you will be noticed.

Humility is not meant for a particular group of people alone. Whether you are rich or poor, humility matters a lot in your life and this attracts love and respect from people around you. It unlocks every potential in you. I am always excited about the humble nature of some people who are truly great achievers. They do not mind the social status of the underprivileged who come close to them, as they freely give them listening ears and even solve their problems. Prince Arthur Eze, the Chairman/CEO of Atlas Oranto Petroleum International Nigeria Limited, displays this attribute that rarely comes from achievers of such magnitude. Despite his enormous wealth, he is not arrogant. People get surprised when they see or meet him, because of his non-sophisticated physical appearance.

His simplicity and meekness clearly demonstrate his openness to people, irrespective of their races or religious inclinations. He welcomes people with open arms, and is always ready to render helping hands. As a true man of the people, he feels obliged to respond to as many invitations as possible, to make his positive contributions. His packages are astonishing, as many common people gain from his benevolence. What gladdens the hearts of many in his character is that he does not like seeing people suffering. With a humble heart, he offers limitless opportunities to people who come in contact with him. The more he humbles himself, the more he is exalted. This is a powerful virtue, worthy of emulation, if we wish to be influential.

Be Willing To Follow Others

Do not insist on you leading all the time. During conversations, be willing to follow another person, even if you do not get to talk about your idea. Just have a listening ear. It makes the other person feel that you are interested in his talks. It is not only your decision that will be upheld all the time. You need to consider the feeling and contributions of others. When necessary, give credit for other's ideas. When you ask others their opinions, they will feel satisfied that you are carrying them along. Some people are never satisfied unless it is their own suggestions that are being carried out. But human beings are meant to understand and follow one another. So, imbibe this quality.

Don't Be Boastful

The need for us not to be boastful about our successes calls our attention. After all, everything we have been able to achieve was made possible by God. We can simply use our achievements to motivate others to work as hard as we have done, to equally give them room to score their own high points. Boasting means that no other person can do that thing except you.

Let us strive to move others into action by letting them know how we registered some successes. That action is not boasting, but inspirational. I remember when I started my driving lesson in Grenoble, France. The person teaching me narrated how he was able to drive perfectly within a period of one week only; he therefore *gingered* me by saying: "if I could do it, then, you can." That threw a challenge to me. I felt I could equally do what my fellow human being did. To me, he was not boasting, but rather, inspiring me to succeed, as he did. So, let our achievements be discussed in such a way that the person listening to us will be moved into working harder. Of course, you can still narrate those achievements in a humble manner, for the message to be well assimilated.

Give Opportunities To Others

Since everyone has his own individual gift, ask others to join in conversations and contribute. Note that your skills can be developed, with the help of others. You have to value other people's time as much as your own, and help them with their goals. Try to rate other people as first, and be less significant. It is disgusting having talks with someone who will never allow others to talk. Get other people's opinions and join to your own, so that you will increase your knowledge. It is wrong to claim to know everything. Of course, it is impossible.

Allow others to praise you, rather than you, praising yourself. As you discuss with others, you need to listen more and talk less. Ensure that the other person is done, during a conversation, before adding your own talks. Do not be carried away by intolerant principles, which may result to explosive reactions. Rather than that, you have to subdue aggression when dealing with others. Teach all that you can, for the benefit of others. They will love you for that. If you recognise the fact that you know little and that there is always more to learn, you will always wish to learn from others.

Pleasant Remarks Are Cherished

How do you feel when you appreciate somebody for a great thing he did for you, and then receive this remark: "It's my pleasure"? Equally, when you invite someone for a little assistance, the person will say: "I'm honoured to render this assistance," *or* "I'm honoured to be invited." That is pure humility, and these are soothing comments from the mouth of a humble person. The practice of the use of such soothing comments will draw a lot of people to you, because, they will feel cherished. Remember that relationship is all about cherishing each other.

Don't Neglect Your Faults

When you recognise that you have faults, admit when you are wrong and accept corrections. Do not answer Mr. 'Incorrigible' or Mrs. 'Incorrigible' Accept new ideas and change, not being stuck on what you knew before. Forgive those who have offended you, and move forward, without revenge. It is human to be wrong, so, admit it when you are wrong.

Criticise Constructively, Don't Condemn

It is wrong to see only faults in other people. Seeking avenues to find weak areas in people is a negative trend, and should not be practised. No one is perfect, therefore, be free to use constructive criticism to make corrections, rather than dampening the morale of someone who has dared initiating an action. This, sometimes, creates the impression that you are not happy with the progress that the person is making.

Do not be a fault finder, be an assistant to someone who is trying to do something. Your own encouragement might make a huge difference. Share your own knowledge to pass on what you have learnt. Appreciate others when they do well, and learn quickly. Criticise less, appreciate more. It is healthier for you.

It Pays To Be Humble

Humility offers social benefits. Humble people, according to studies, are more effective leaders, and are valued in social settings, due to their tendency to behave more generously and selflessly. It brings about excellence in leadership, as humble leaders are not only better liked, but are more effective. They make better managers and better employees, and this results to better work performance. Humility enables freedom. It means learning to value yourself in a way that is not dependent on outperforming other people, and being the best at things you do. It allows you to feel okay with yourself as someone who is ordinary or average. It soothes the soul.

It brings about higher self-control. Studies indicate that humble people have high self-control, which is a successful key in life. It gives an individual an honest and accurate sense of which areas that truly need to be improved. This creates self-awareness, as the person will come to terms with his true personality. Better relationships are equally brought about by humility.

Humility promotes learning and growth, because, one will be open to new possibilities. Students in a classroom, or people learning to live better lives, cannot open to new experiences if they lack humility, as they believe they already know everything they need to. When they open to new experiences, there will be record of higher grades.

The importance of humility cannot be overemphasised, as Rick Pitino, an American basketball coach who has achieved a measure of success as an author and a motivational speaker, states: "Humility is the true key to success. Successful people lose their way at times. They often embrace and overindulge from the fruits of success. Humility halts this arrogance and self-indulging trap. Humble people share the credit and wealth, remaining focused and hungry to continue the journey of success." Surely, humility pays.

~ What Am I? ~

1. Bringing myself to lowliness
Draws me closer to holiness
Realising that I am mere sand
Operating on bare ground.

2. Rating me as being superior
Rather makes me to feel inferior
'Nothing is gained by arrogance
I still crave for relevance.

3. I need to be pursuing
All things that need reviewing
I might stumble
I will stay humble, and never grumble

4. Why should I be boastful
When life's gain can only come from
the hopeful?
Life demands much tolerance
To bring out the best performance.

5. A humble living, I admire
To reach the peak, I aspire
To get that cherished quality
Through my dear life of jollity.

Chapter 17
Initiate A Selling Point

S elling point is a unique quality in you that will attract people to you. It is certain that it is an advantageous feature that appeals to the prospective buyer of a service, product, and the like, but it is not only in business that you can devise selling point strategies, like making your goods to be of better quality, making them cheaper, making them easily available, and so on. You can equally advertise your trait in such a way that people will get attracted to you. Your personality matters a lot, and a well-groomed personality is the key to success.

You need to make yourself more relevant, because, relevance is the only job security that exists in today's uncertain business world. The tsunami of change is hitting everyone. We live in a time of vast and uneasy change, where economic, social and political turmoil has become the order of the day. To be relevant means you have to be an integral part of your organisation, company, economy, and environment. You will be the kind of person on whom others depend, whether for leadership, expertise, acumen or emotional support. You will be valued. Identifying and making optimal use of your special trait will be a selling point for you, if objectively utilised. Your selling point is your own power.

What Do You Wish To Sell?

It is yourself you wish to put up for grabs. You wish to highlight your strengths and special attributes, for others to cherish and consequently, make you excel in life. Your selling point may be your specialty, or it may be a perceived difference that may be appealing to someone. Your moral disposition may be your selling point. A situation may arise when they will need people of your character. You will be taken up.

There are traits that need to be upheld and even used as selling points, for example - politeness, generosity, fairness, honesty, loyalty, humour, compassion, patience, courage, and so on. A generous person, for instance, stands tall in his community. People always prefer the company of a generous giver to the company of a selfish hoarder. People are naturally attracted towards others who have an open heart to share with others. In fact, this is a great selling point! Generosity, in turn, makes the person happier and healthier. It equally increases your life satisfaction, improves your relationship with others, and alleviates fear. When we share what we have, we feel our abundance, it becomes real to us, and that diminishes our fears.

Another great selling point is humour. There is a saying that 'laughter is the best medicine'. If you can initiate this as your selling point, then, your relationship with others will be enhanced. With your ability to make others laugh, you will be much empowered to heal and renew, because, this is a tremendous resource for surmounting problems and supporting both physical and emotional health. As Paul E. McGhee stated: "Your sense of humour is one of the most powerful tools you have to make certain that your daily mood and emotional state support good health." McGhee, President of the Laughter Remedy, Montclair, New Jersey, was a pioneer in humour research, laying the ground work for the current interest in the health benefits of humour, and internationally known for his own humour research. Come on, supporter of good health, do not relent.

Loyalty is a great virtue that people, especially in the offices, adore. It simply means faithfulness to a person or cause. Anyone with this special attribute is easily attracted to the boss. You may be put in a certain advantaged position because of the fact that you do not disobey the constituted authority. Many people have used this trait to excel in their jobs. Loyalty is a strong bond. Research has shown that employees, who are loyal and remain faithful in their jobs, are more productive. This explains why employers have much flair for loyalty. This can definitely turn to be a great selling point for someone, as well.

The saying that 'honesty is the best policy', brings us to understand that this virtue can make a wonderful selling point to someone. The fact that you will always stand for the truth, will definitely ignite a strong relationship between you and others around you. This means that you will be trusted and can be a confidant. You will be dependable. We all know that human beings need people to trust, people they can rely on, people who are courageous to tell them the truth. This is why honesty can develop into an enviable selling point to someone.

Apart from the traits mentioned above, there are others you can initiate, and you will be good to go. Your decision takes you to your goal. The choice is entirely yours. I believe that everyone has one or more positive traits to sell out to people, which, in turn, will contribute to making the world a better place to live in. Your personality is entirely up to you. Your decisions and actions are the determinant factors of your personality. The only way to change your personality is to take active steps to become the person you want to be.

Necessary Steps To Take

Before you can initiate an acceptable selling point, you have to, first of all, list out the characteristics that describe you. From the list, you can conveniently select the one that is most appropriate for any particular situation. Check the skills and experience you have. These will determine your ability to take up a particular selling point you wish to initiate. Find out who you are at the deepest level. You need to appear to others as you are, without pretence. If you do not understand who you are, and where you are coming from, you cannot lead or influence others.

Take action to change you and change the world. Without action, even a great and brilliant mind remains entirely irrelevant. Identify aspects of your life that others around do not have. Groom them to perfection in such a way that people will be attracted to you. A great way to become well-rounded to improve your personality is by taking a hobby. Many hobbies exist, ranging from crafts, arts, sports, volunteering and writing. As a matter of fact, reading a book can push you to be better.

You should recognise and share feelings (such as sadness or happiness) being experienced by another person. You should have the desire to help others and to care for them. This is relevant, because it creates the deep connection that brings people together.

Mastery is essential because, if you are not competent in what you wish to uphold as a selling point, you cannot be useful to others. You can achieve mastery through a process of continuous improvement of your talents and abilities. This requires the ability to put first things first, and to stay mindful while taking action. Of course, this requires a clear view of reality, a willingness to get beyond deeply rooted beliefs, awareness of your subconscious desires, and commitment to truth. According to Frank Zappa, "Art is making something out of nothing, and selling it." Zappa was a self-taught composer and performer, a highly productive and prolific artist. He remained a major influence on musicians and composers. You can think of something that is completely new, and generate a new idea from there with a view to creating a great selling point.

No Room For Negative Traits

You cannot expect to live a positive life if you hang with negative people, as Joel Osteen observes. No negative character poses as a selling point. For instance, if you are a cheat, nobody likes to be cheated. This is because cheating destroys life. Cheating in academics, business, or social life, is never a tolerable act. Once you are found to be a cheat, people will be harsh on you, and no one can trust you, even when you try to do the right thing. Cheating can lead to financial ruin, family ruin, and shunning by others. People will avoid and reject you.

How does it feel being near an antagonistic person? Irritating, right? There is no way people will be endeared to someone who is antagonistic, because, he will always be hostile and disputing with others. This results to low turnout of productivity. This trait is quite repellent, rather than attractive. Avoid antagonism if you are to be considered and revered by others. If you are hot-tempered, people will run away from you, so, anger should be cast away from you, for people to be endeared to you. One who is hot-tempered is one who is quick to anger or who does not control his emotions very well. It is a bad trait and can never project you positively.

You need to flee from avarice, if you do not want people to run away from you. This act is an insatiable greed for riches; inordinate, miserly desire to gain and hoard wealth. Anyone who is avaricious has the tendency of looking for ways of looting an organisation's treasury. Since he is insatiable, he is never content with what he has. Generally, people dislike associating with such persons. It is not a selling point at all.

I have not yet seen people who feel comfortable with cowards. Cowardice is lack of courage. It also means timidity. Finally, it is a brutal conduct towards the weak or undefended. This is a negative trait, when it comes to social acceptability. Since success demands taking risks, how can a coward venture into risk-taking? The heroic acts are simply impossible for him, as he will, under no circumstances, endanger himself, and may even betray close friends and family in an effort to save himself from being harmed. So, being cowardly can never be a selling point.

A child who is notoriously stubborn can never be accepted or welcomed by anyone. What does it cost to be simply obedient? Thomas S. Monson, an American religious leader and author, stated: "The great test of this life is obedience." This brings peace of mind. It brings happy relationship in the family, at the workplace, and with God. This goes to explain that stubbornness does us much harm. It can never make one to be popular; rather, it brings scorn and curses.

The practice of smoking is not a good trait, because of its negative effects on the body, especially, the heart. It does not portray someone positively, too. People may identify you as 'that man who smokes more than three packets of cigarettes everyday'. A nice opportunity may come, but, due to your smoking habit, it may be given to another person who will not have the tendency of 'burning sticks' inside his office. No wonder hotels tag some rooms as 'non-smoking' rooms. This is to demonstrate how unacceptable this trait is.

Rudeness is another negative trait. This is an act of being discourteous, impolite, uncultured, rough, harsh, or ungentle. This calls for serious concern. People will detest you when you display such trait. You will be unbearable and intolerable. In fact, Bryant McGill asserts "No one is more insufferable than he who lacks basic courtesy." McGill is an American author, aphorist, and speaker in the fields of self-development, personal freedom, and human rights. The list of negative traits is endless, so, brush aside any one of them you have been nursing, and bring out the positive ones, so that you can proudly choose one that will be your selling point.

Your Attitude Matters

You cannot initiate a selling point when you are having a bad day. Everything boils down to your attitude towards life. Every day, we have a choice about how we see the world. We can open our eyes wide with wonder, and decide to be amazed and thankful, or, we can choose to approach life with dampened spirit: with our eyes half-closed, we see only the worst in people, circumstances and situations. Every natural course, including the timing for everything, has to go through the same process. The only difference is how we approach it. Making every situation dramatic does not make it easier to deal with. A child may drop a cup on the ground, one may shout: "why are you playing with that cup?" Another person may simply smile, and say: "I hope you're enjoying yourself over there." You may be caught in the rain and may start cursing God for sending the rain to pour on you, while another person may feel the touch of the drops and start enjoying the sensations.

Your attitude is simply your mental outlook on circumstances: your temperament, mood, or viewpoint. It is a powerful sentiment, and it affects every part of your life - self-image, relationships, business, and, even your health. This attribute is a key component in defining one's personality. It affects how people see you – whether they like or dislike you, whether they want to be around you or avoid you, whether you gain or lose influence with them. It is reflected through the tone of your voice, the expression on your face, and your body language. Examine yourself to know if your attitude is hurting or helping you. If your family, friends and co-workers were to describe your attitude, what would they say? If you were an employer of labour, would you go for someone with good attitude or bad one?

Try to learn from your failures, and stop complaining. Force yourself to stop thinking about them. Continuing to think about mistakes you have made will affect your self-esteem, self-confidence, and ultimately, your attitude. Your success does not depend on how often you fall, but on how often you get up and try again; on how much you learn from each experience. If you complain from the beginning of your problem to the end, you cannot change the situation, rather, you are' aggravating issues, therefore, no progress or improvement will be made. Most people do not want to be around those who complain.

Your attitude is a choice, and that choice is 100% within your control. The choice you make will influence every aspect of your life. Changing your attitude changes everything. When you find yourself in an unpleasant situation, complaints and nagging cannot solve problems, as they will only make time drag on. Just resort to either singing or even humming your favourite song. That does the magic of relief from anger and frustration. Be a pleasant person, to enable you unfold your heart's needs. Once you are able to understand your personal traits, you are on your great way to start the journey into self-discovery.

Your Selling Point Distinguishes You From Others.

Being distinguished is really good. Distinguished people have impressive reputation to match. This is a state of having an air of distinction, dignity, or eminence. When you are distinguished, you will have more connections, admirers and self-confidence, to pursue whatever goal you have in life. The particular trait you have chosen to uphold as your selling point, if well-developed, will make you well-known and respected, especially for achievement in that particular field.

~ You Are Unique ~

1. You are equipped to be a champion
And not to be a mere onion
You're here with specific vision
To come and achieve your mission.

2. An urgent call to be familiar
With things that make you peculiar
Avoid what makes you unfamiliar
strive not to be a liar.

3. If life should be so hilarious
You have to become very humorous
For your own fans to be numerous
As your actions are so marvellous.

4. To deeply express our passion
We have to show compassion
In an acceptable fashion
To reflect our sincere action.

5. You don't need a big boutique
To showcase your own technique
Flee completely from antique
Because you are quite unique.

Chapter 18

Flee From Idleness

Idleness, which is a state of not being occupied, is a negative trait that can deny someone a huge opportunity for greatness in life. It is an ill wind that blows no one any good. It destroys the souls of many, due to its resultant negative consequences. It retards the positive functionality of the brain. It comes up with many evil thoughts. A popular Italian painter, sculptor, and architect, Leonardo Da Vinci, shared his view thus: "Just as iron rusts from disuse; even so does inaction spoil the intellect." The body is like a machine which needs constant servicing, to perform optimally.

Idleness does not only tempt us to sin, but it causes a lot of sins and even, depression. It is when we are idle that we feel bored and tend to eat too much, gossip with people, sit too much on the videos, recount old memories, complain of bad moods, and equally, think of committing one negative action or the other, as the saying goes: "the idle mind is the devil's workshop." You need to make great use of your intellect in any way you find yourself disposed to do so. Idleness is a strong enemy in one's bid to empower himself with his own natural gift.

Watch Out For Signs Of Idleness

Many a time, we find ourselves neglecting what we are expected to do at a particular time. Equally, we find ourselves 'trapped' in doing the things we are not expected to do at that particular point in time. People who usually fall victims of such are those who never make plans. Lack of plan of action can seriously lead to idleness.

Many instances of idleness exist. When you see yourself sleeping too much, for instance, when others are either reading or working, it is a sign of being idle. The hours of unnecessary sleep you wasted would have been used for positive productivity by you. Of course, when you are tired, you are expected to rest and sleep, because the body needs rest, after exerting much energy. However, too much sleep can deny you of some other vital things, because idleness has set in.

Some people are engulfed in random browsing, without any specific aim. They are simply 'busy' wasting their precious time they would have channelled into more useful ventures. Both students and some other adults are guilty of this, and this negative trend is eating deep into the society. I do not see why a child in the secondary school should be browsing areas which are morally forbidden for him at that stage. If that child had picked up a novel to read, or engaged himself in an intellectual work that would make him grow, he cannot be said to be idle.

Gossiping is another sign that will prove to you that you are idle. If your mind is preoccupied with some work, you will not have time to be gossiping about another person. Of what good is it to sit on somebody's character, either to assassinate the character or destroy your own soul because of your evil thoughts? Some people cannot stay put in their houses, because of their love for gossip. Their children may not even have food on the table, but those people are negatively engaged in discussing people. Little wonder that Eleanor Roosevelt, former First Lady of the United States of America, an extraordinary and controversial First Lady, known for her outspokenness; and the first First Lady to hold her own press conferences, clearly stated: "Great minds discuss ideas; average minds discuss events; small minds discuss people."

As soon as you notice that you are putting off what you can conveniently do now till later, you are displaying signs of idleness. Procrastination is not in the dictionary of hardworking people. They try to carry out their plans as at when due. In the office set up, there may be piles of untreated files, but the boss may be the idle type. This practice of leaving files for a long period of time, delays the implementation of some actions which will move the office forward. So, when you see a lot of untreated files in an office, the officer in charge is simply being idle and lazy.

In the school system, the teacher who is reluctant to go and teach at the right time is displaying an element of idleness. This is to the detriment of the students. In the hospital, a nurse and a doctor who are idle are leaving their patients to fate. When you hear your inner mind talking to you about going to steal from someone, that is a sign that your mind is idle at that time. Ordinarily, you should be thinking of how to make your life better, rather than thinking of going to harm someone else. This is a sign that idleness has set in. In fact, idleness can be seen in all spheres of life, and in all actions expected from human beings. So, we simply need to watch out, to know when we are idle. It is an ill wind that blows no good to humanity.

Getting Engaged Makes You Healthy And Fit

Getting involved in sporting activities can remove the spirit of idleness in you. This is because sports make you to be healthy and fit, paving way for positive thinking. Sports are really entertaining, as they catch our attention to give us pleasure as much as we need. Some life conditions may overwhelm us, and naturally, make us downcast and unhappy, but as soon as we get engaged in a sporting activity, we are motivated and refreshed.

You have to choose a particular sporting activity that appeals to you, and you will witness the magic that will make you shout: "Oh! la la." Aerobics, for instance, gives me joy and much fun. It is a form of physical exercise that combines rhythm with stretching and strength-training routines, with the goal of improving all elements of fitness. The music that accompanies it always puts me in high spirit, and I can go any length to express my joy during the exercise. After aerobics and cycling exercises, I feel real good! A little visit to the gym from time to time, performs a lot of magic in your body fitness exploits. At home too, you can go on choreography and other leisure games, with your family members.

Some other people may be interested in football, while others may be interested in table tennis, athletics, volleyball, and the like. The choice is yours, but, be assured that all are good, to put you on the right frame of mind. Just have your fun to the point of people asking you: "*qu'est-ce qui se passe?*" ("What's happening?"), and "*qu'est-ce que c'est?*" ("What is it?").

To quote Brian Tracy, a successful speaker, writer, and entrepreneur, and who is one of America's leading writers and speakers on personal development, self improvement, time management, goal-setting, and a host of other success topics, "the potential of the average person is like a huge ocean unsailed, a new continent unexplored, a world of possibilities waiting to be released and channelled toward some great goal." When you are engaged in activities that interest you, you will live healthily, because you will always be living with a feeling of self-satisfaction. This state of mind will drive off worries and unpleasant thoughts from your mind. The feeling of happiness will always be experienced and this, in turn, makes your blood flow freely and smoothly. It will be difficult for you to be downcast, as idleness can cause sickness. I detest dull moments! If you have something doing, you will feel your mind is getting positively focused and, of course, that earns you healthy psychological living.

Value Your Time

Try to fight against procrastination so that you can easily attain your potential. Philip Stanhope, 4th Earl of Chesterfield advises: "know the true value of time: snatch, seize, and enjoy every moment of it. No idleness, laziness, no procrastination: never put till tomorrow what you can do today." I believe that the value of time needs to be cherished by all, so that idleness will be completely eradicated.

However, we need to note here that relaxation does not mean idleness. There is definitely time for everything: time to work and time to relax. All work and no play, it is often said, makes Jack a dull boy. We should always take time to relax, when need be, so that our nerves can rest a little, before more energy will be used. In John Lubbock's book, *The Use of Life*, he stated: "Rest is not idleness, and to lie on the grass under trees on a summer's day, listening to the murmur of the water, or watching the clouds float across the sky, is by no means, a waste of time." Let us always get it right, by allotting time to our various activities, so that the body system will be balanced and said to be in a healthy state.

When you make a good scheduling of time, you can never be idle. You will either be engaged in doing some work, or engaged in relaxing. With your time schedule, you will know what you can realistically achieve, know how you can plan for the unexpected, provide time for essential tasks, work on your personal and career goals, and have enough time for family, friends, exercises, and hobbies. Once you give yourself a time goal to complete a particular task, you are equipping yourself with healthy tips for life. Time, when valued, removes stress and anxiety from you. This is because you will find freedom from deadline pressure and from general stress. This will result to more productivity, less procrastination, and much more availability of time to relax. There is time for everything, indeed.

Do Not Leave The Iron To Rust

If you do not want to be weak in thoughts, get yourself busy, just as Ezra Cornell, an American capitalist and philanthropist, founder of Cornell University, said: "Idleness is to the human mind like rust to iron." When iron is not put into use, there is the tendency for it to rust. Equally, the human mind depreciates in quality, when it is not allowed to function effectively.

Corrosion, which is the deterioration of a metal as a result of chemical reactions between it and the surrounding environment, can be equated with the deterioration of the human mind which is not allowed to function effectively. However, preventive measures against corrosion, such as environmental modifications, coating, plating, and so on, are really working. In the same way, fleeing from idleness plays a tremendous role in rescuing the human mind from decay. In fact, idleness is a disease, and should not be allowed to flow in our veins.

Develop Passions For Great Deeds

We should not allow our interests or passions to die. It is through the determination of developing such that we can record great deeds. If, for instance, you have passion for writing, what prevents you from doing so? If you have passion for painting, of what use are you when you are not engaged in such? You may be interested in photography, then, get a camera, and learn how to use it. Snap pictures at will. Take all kinds of pictures, whether at home or at events. Your skill in that will be fully developed. Some are gifted in teaching others. They should equally develop that by engaging in teaching children and other social groups. If you leave what you have, it slips off from your hands. You need to make great use of your intellect in any way you find yourself disposed to do so.

I have seen people who are talented in sculpting, and who have put this talent into use. Today, they are great sculptors. Some others who have seen themselves excelling in music have developed their interest in that on a higher scale. Consequently, they are recording success. One thing is to recognise great deeds, but, another is to develop passions to attain such. You need to find your passion and develop it into a real goal. Know your skills and aptitudes. However, for you to meaningfully develop your passion, you need to set specific goal so that you will work towards that. By having a specific objective, you are set to accomplish that within a target time.

Consequences Of Idleness

Definitely, an idle person should know that he is prone to many negative consequences. Idleness provokes a lot of regrets in life, and this lowers self-esteem. The idle person finds himself giving up easily, with little or no efforts about doing something. This results to lack of production. This can also cause irritability. It is irritating for one to see himself idle, when his mates are busy accomplishing much. He feels depressed too, as a result of non-achievement. Depression, in turn, causes deteriorating health conditions. Really, poor state of health calls for serious concern.

Idleness can cause obesity, which is a very serious threat to life. As long as one does not engage himself meaningfully, calories will accumulate in the body system, and there is the tendency for one to develop one kind of health threat or the other, in his life. When one is largely inactive, the stored caloric energy turns to fat. Sometimes, cardiovascular disease sets in.

One of the greatest sins is the sin of leaving undone those things which we ought to have done. Sometimes, out of idleness or laziness, a husband cannot feign for the family. Out of idleness, the wife cannot take care of the children and the husband. Out of idleness, a student fails to perform well in the exams. An idle administrator cannot make an organisation or school to grow. Sometimes, an idle person finds himself in the list of people on hunger threat due to the fact that he is lazy to go to the farm, and even to cook. He eats more of junk food than engaging in the real nutrition. He suffers social disconnect. He is unable to have meaningful contacts with friends and other associates, because he is most of the time, on his own. Incidentally, without socialisation, much cannot be achieved. Most of the time, he finds himself guilty of not performing the desired tasks.

Overcoming Idleness

The ideal way of overcoming idleness is to think about the drastic consequences. When you think about what will happen when you display the signs of idleness, then you will surely decide to start engaging yourself with meaningful actions. Many people have remained ordinary because they fail to make conscientious efforts to improve their life patterns. You have to make attempt to move from where you are, so that you can move forward.

Get some achievable goals so that you will have something to look forward to. They should be things that will interest you. You can equally make a year planner which you will try to follow. It will help you not to be idle. If you are not naturally inspired, think of what you can change in your routine. The routine may vary from your food or actions. You will surely get something that moves you into action, so that you will not just stay without active moments.

Exercise regularly so that your brain will always be ready to accommodate your thoughts. You will, through exercises, have a healthy living. Keep on reminding yourself that you can do something. Positive affirmation helps you flee from idleness, because you are determined to move forward. Of course, action changes everything. Exercises make you feel more energised, as they get your blood flowing.

Punctuality, it is said, is the soul of business. You have to form the habit of waking up early, to look for something doing. Sleeping too much can never help you. Sleep is meant to revive the hard-working person so that he can return renewed to work. So, to avoid idleness, you should not be glued to your bed.

You should be mindful of the fact that life is not always easy, unless you want to be unrealistic. Life is full of difficulties, as well as excitements, but most importantly, filled with hope. Therefore, being idle will mean that you do not wish to move on with life, and that can be self-destructive. All you need to do is to change your attitude for the better, so that you can enjoy the life's benefits, as it has a lot to offer.

~ Rescued From The Pit ~

1. This dungeon gets me unoccupied
   When I crave to be occupied
   Nothing bugs me like inaction
   When there is room for attraction.

2. Rescue me from being wrapped
   In this darkness where I'm trapped
   My life, you want to annihilate
   But no, I'll surely emancipate.

3. How can I be so redundant
   When opportunities are abundant?
   You can never get me caged
   Nor let me be enraged.

4. I'm out and never downcast
   Because I'm not an outcast
   No matter your tricky surprises
   I'm filled with many enterprises.

5. You can't get me depressed
   I'll rather be refreshed
   When you are so unjust
   Resistance is a must.

Chapter 19

Advocate Of Optimism

Optimism is a disposition to take a bright, hopeful view of things. It is also a tendency to look on the more favourable side of events or conditions, and to expect the most favourable outcome. For one to succeed in life, and make his gift his power, he needs to see the possibility in what he wishes to achieve. Samuel Johnson, an English writer and critic, and one of the most famous literary figures of the 18th Century, whose best known work is his 'Dictionary of the English Language', wrote: "The habit of looking on the bright side of every event is worth more than a thousand pounds a year."

I do not know why some people will never see anything good in life. Every situation, to them, is calamitous. They do not ever think that things will be better. Their whole ideas and discussions are always negative. They get involved in such, because they have failed to be optimistic. Such people fail when they venture into some business deal or new creative task. They simply say: "I don't think it will work." They lose hope about every opportunity, always embracing failure which, they, through their attitudes, invite.

This attitude of always assuming the worst can have major negative consequences on your life. If you see only the negative aspect of any situation, you are inviting problems to your life, because, you may develop chronic illnesses later on in life. That will make you miss opportunities, fail to take actions that would be necessary to improve your quality of life, and even neglect problems that need to be solved. If you are optimistic, you will always look for light at the end of the tunnel. You will always see the glass as 'half full', not 'half empty'. In fact, you will see yourself doing what you are always dreaming of, and, consequently, empowering yourself with the talent you possess.

Peace Of Mind

When your mind is at peace, then you can easily go to bed and sleep. Target peace of mind each day, so that your body can never be stressed up. Remember that when the mind is upset, ugly sickness finds a way of paving in. Resist that by having peace of mind. Stop over thinking. Over thinking is to analyse something too much, not thinking about anything else. It will affect your life in a negative way. As soon as you notice that you are over thinking, direct your attention elsewhere, to distract your mind. This is the period your hobby equally comes to play. Once you get involved in one of your favourite activities, the over thinking you were involved in will gradually disappear. Exercises like jogging, cycling, tennis, can help during those moments.

Another way to have peace of mind is to ease your expectations. Learn to accept things as they come to you, not expecting them to be always exactly how you want them. One man was thinking he would win a particular award, but incidentally, his mate won it. Being an advocate of optimism, he just accepted it that way, without grudges.

What gives Mr. 'A' peace of mind may not be exactly what gives Mr. 'B' same thing. It is left to you to know what you enjoy doing. Get on with it and you will have peace of mind. According to Robert Alan, an American screen writer, director, and producer, "We can only help make our lives and our world more peaceful, when we, ourselves feel peace. Peace already exists within each of us, if we only allow ourselves to feel its comfort. Peace of mind begins when we stop thinking about how far we have to go, or how hard the road has been, and just let ourselves feel peace. Peace of mind gives us the strength to keep trying and keep working along the path that we KNOW is right for our lives." Peace!!!

A Little Smile A Day
Smiling is the human's most powerful gesture, and it can never hurt! I know of a lady whose disposition is always in the smiling mood. And whenever she smiles, everyone around her smiles too or even laughs. The result is that people are automatically happy, and this brings joy. An optimistic person is often found smiling, no matter the circumstance. Your smile can brighten someone's day, because it is contagious, so to say. Smiling is a good start if you want more happiness and joy. It directly affects your brain, thus making your mindset shift easier. Relationships are definitely built on smiles, so, to retain a genuine relationship, do not let your face get dim. Smile to encourage trust and to build on your social health.

I wonder how some people feel okay, without a little smile. Smile acts as a catalyst in releasing low tension in tensed up situations. Since smiling puts you in a right position tone for the day, why not embrace it fully? It costs nothing. When you are overwhelmed with situations, the best resort is to put up a smile, to pursue the anxiety, frustration, and worries. If you get angry when you are worried and frustrated, then it is like pouring fuel inside fire. This will be dangerous to your health, and can simply worsen the situation in which you find yourself.

Do you wonder why some people are more productive than others? A little secret, you may say - smile. The 'whistle while we work' mentality is working. As joy is brought into your heart when you are exercising a particular task, you will be moved to go further. For me, smiling makes me feel 'high', and that is when you will get the best from me. Studies have shown that those who smile earn more success, as they are easily approached with business ideas. Nobody would naturally love to do anything with someone who always frowns his face. Open up, and put a smile on that face and get what you want. As Dr T. P. Chia, a Singaporean former political prisoner, says, "A smiling face is a beautiful face. A smiling heart is a happy heart."

Smiling makes people more attractive. Imagine going to meet a lady and suddenly, she turns you off with a hiss! Imagine the embarrassment. On the other hand, a lady who beams with smiles will attract people with good intentions. Looking younger is equally one of the resultant effects of smiles, because the face is naturally lifted. As the body relaxes through smiling, most of the negative traits of life are likely to keep at bay.

Some people spend a lot of money seeking good health, and trying to boost their health. Some visit doctors regularly, buy supplements, go for fitness routines, and enrol in gym memberships, all in the name of making their health better. These, they do, without knowing that the easiest and cheapest ways to boost their health, their longevity, their mood, and even their success, is to smile. Complaints of high blood pressure have natural temporary approach to the reduction of such - a smile. This slows the heart and relaxes the body. Every problem cannot be controlled by drugs alone, some can be approached through the ways we carry ourselves. So, smile and kill pain. It is simply a natural pain killer.

Don't Live In The Past

You need to realise that you can change your past, by creating a new history. If you carry over any emotional pain into your new experiences and may be, relationships, you are likely to cause problems for yourself, without any conscious desire. You cannot change it physically, but you can change the way you perceive it. Any ugly experience you have had in the past should be taken up by you as a motivation to change your future. You may be thrown off a particular job, that is the time for you to even think of something that would have been better for you all these years. A particular business of yours might have been booming, only for it to flop suddenly, that is simply a signal for you to think of something else for your great heart. Stop lamenting on how much better things used to be, because you are a creative, innovative, adaptable human being, capable of making the choice to live better.

If, on the other hand, you have been having an immoral standard of living in the past, and you wish to move forward, leave the old stuff and any other thing that is related with your dim past completely, otherwise, you will always be tied to your past. It is never good to pour out spit and go back to lick it. *A Dieu ne plaise!* (God forbid!)

Definitely, you have to create new ideas and make new friends, as you break contact with all those who wanted to ruin your life in the past. As a matter of fact, the ones who wasted your life in the past would never wish you to succeed, so you just have to break contact with all of them, to pave way for a breath of fresh air into your life. The memory of an unhappy childhood or wretched family background should not be allowed to destroy your current chances of living a fulfilled life.

Remove the past from your future, and create a positive future. Moving with the realisation that the past is already gone, and that the future is yet unwritten, will put you in a better mood to develop a forward-focused you. Whether it is the traumatic experience of losing someone dear to you, or being rejected in a close relationship, or thrown out of a job you cherish, or missing a very important appointment, your new policy should be: 'Forward, ever; backward, never'. Just as Terri Guillemets advises us: "Don't let the past steal your present." Terri Guillemets, is a quotation anthologist from Phoenix, Arizona, who has collected quotes since age thirteen. Her passion is sharing literary, inspirational, thought-provoking, and humorous quotations with a worldwide audience via her website The Quote Garden at www.quotegarden.com, one of the most long-standing online quotation collections, and the first to offer a wide variety of special occasion topics.

Use Positive Affirmations

Being optimistic in life, demands positive affirmations. Affirmation is the act of expressing agreement with or commitment to something. I normally hear people say that there is power in the tongue. What you declare usually manifests in one way or the other. Here, we need to make positive affirmations pertaining our lives and what we want to achieve. This is evidence of optimism.

In times of anxiety, self-esteem, healing, stress, and so on, you can make positive affirmations. These are ways you use to make the situations look lighter than they really are. Some instances of positive affirmations are: "I can control my attitude toward life"; "I create my circumstances"; "Anything is possible"; "I choose to live my positive side of life"; "I always have a choice"; "Yes! I can." Positive affirmations will definitely make you feel better about yourself and your life. Your way of negative thinking and unbelief in yourself will be changed through this practice. The type of life you have always wanted for yourself will be achieved.

Positive affirmations work, and they can be used to manifest your needs, and also to bring positive and permanent changes to your life. The use of these affirmations force you to keep focused on your inner goal. If, for instance, you affirm thus: "I shall pass my exams with 5 Distinctions and 3 credits," you have already declared it, and so, your thoughts and efforts will automatically channel you to attain the manifestation of that proclamation. One man affirmed that he would finish his house in the village within one year, no matter the distractions. With the spirit of commitment to his positive affirmation, the task has been accomplished. He is happily living there with his family members.

One of the most powerful life strategies is developing a positive mindset. This can make you achieve whatever you want. Professionals and business people can use these techniques to develop personal power, or gain a competitive edge. In fact, at a personal level, your life and your health will be transformed. Equally, your joy and passion for life will be renewed, because, you will wake up each morning with excitement, energy, and joy for the new day. With the power of positive affirmation, you can turn failure around into success, because this positive attitude is the fuel to your success - success in academics, success in business, success in your political career, success in all life's ventures. You can make your dreams come through.

Compliment Others

You need to think well of others, and move a step further to compliment them, if you desire to be reckoned with. An optimistic person finds it easy to do this. How do you feel when you receive compliments like: "You look good"; "you're great in music"; "Oh, I like your type of earrings"; "You really look sweet today"; "Your suit fits you"; "Your hair looks amazing"; You're such a good friend"; Your writing is impressive"; "I love your performance"; "You are a genius"; "You have a lovely house"? You feel great, right? Can you equally spread that love and give that feeling to others? You have to genuinely appreciate other people, through active interest in them. Mark Twain, author and humorist, one of America's best known writers, and lauded as the 'greatest

American humorist of his age', affirmed it thus: "I can live for two months on a good compliment." That is the power of compliments.

Compliments build trust. Someone around you may be so shy that no one ever notices him. Consequently, he buries his thoughts in his hearts, and never makes attempts to answer questions in the class or makes contributions during meetings. You may be the one to bring him out from the cocoon, through your sincere compliments such as: "You're really doing better"; and "I like the way you reason". After all, everyone has the desire to be acknowledged, and definitely, by building others, we are building ourselves. Someone may confidently walk to you and pay you a compliment thus: "You're great in noticing good things in people." What goes around, they say, comes around.

Compliments bring more productivity. If someone notices you, there is the tendency for you to bring out the better part of you. So, this is a vital ingredient to achieve success - paying compliments. It is sad to note that, sometimes, some good things go unacknowledged. People are experts in pointing out what is wrong with something or someone, while taking for granted, what is right. A great compliment is about acknowledging the positives about another person.

For me, each time my husband compliments me on my dressing or general appearance, I feel I am in the seventh heaven of happiness. That uplifts my mood for the day. You know what it means for a lady to receive compliment on her dressing or general appearance. It sounds great really when I hear: "You're looking cute today"; "This cloth really fits you"; "I love your hairstyle". Equally, as a woman cooking food for the family, what compliment can be better than: "Oh! Your food is really delicious"? It is an indirect way of telling you to maintain the standard, and, most importantly, encouraging you to do more, while acknowledging your efforts. So, naturally, I will strive to be in the mood of receiving more compliments, because, that makes my day. Stop feeling that someone's head will 'swell up' because of your compliment; dish it out, and get personality improvement from people you come in contact with. Help improve others through your motivational compliments. Do not be a miser of good wishes, so that you will equally be wished well. "One good turn," they say, "deserves another."

Compliments should come from a place of genuine desire to make other people feel better. When you compliment others, you improve your relationships, it makes you happier, you build your self-esteem, you make new friends, you make someone else's day, and they make your own. Compliments can revolutionise how people feel about you, because, they will see you as someone cherishing other people. A powerful compliment is a gift you give to others. It is a way of expressing gratitude and goodwill in the world. Leo Buscaglia observes thus: "Too often we underestimate the power of a touch, a smile, a kind word, a listening ear, an honest compliment, or the smallest act of caring, all of which have the potential to turn a life around." Buscaglia, also known as 'Dr. Love', was an American author, and motivational speaker. He has been called the 'granddaddy of motivational speakers' on television. He was a popular guest on television talk shows, as well as in the lecture circuit.

Better Coping Skills

Being optimistic earns you the ability to cope with situations that may seem too challenging to you. This, of course, will result to your better psychological and physical wellbeing. Positive coping strategies can help with increasing confidence, temporary stress relief, long term stress relief, tackling challenges, increasing motivation. Some of the coping strategies include: learning to forgive, turning to someone you trust, learning how to set goals, building your gratitude, relaxation, reducing your load, and overcoming negative patterns of thinking, through self-assessment.

Enumerate Your Blessings

Each time we sit down to recount what we have been blessed with; our hearts are filled with joy and happiness. This is one of the big deals in life if you want to enrol yourself in the list of successful people. You have succeeded in many areas, therefore, count those blessings, and you will start thinking of organising a powerful thanksgiving in you place of worship. A line in one of our popular songs says: "…when you are discouraged, thinking all is lost…" The next line proffers a solution thus: "count your many blessings, name them one by one." This line is followed by what your reaction would be: "And it will surprise you what that the Lord has done."

Counting your blessings is a secret to more joyful and generous giving and living. Minimise complaints, and constantly remind yourself of the numerous blessings you have, so that you will continue to stay positive. William Penn says: "the secret of happiness is to count your blessings while others are adding up their troubles." This philosopher, who was born in London, was an English real estate entrepreneur, early Quaker (member of a family of religious movements collectively known as the Religious Society of Friends), and the founder of the Province of Pennsylvania, the English North American colony. He was a man of profound religious convictions, who was imprisoned several times in the Tower of London, due to his faith, and his book, *No Cross, No Crown* (1669), written in prison, has become a Christian classic. He was the first great hero of American liberty.

Counting of blessings is an antidote to negative emotions, a neutraliser of envy, avarice, hostility, worry and irritation. How do you feel when you negate the feeling of not having a car, for instance, with the feeling that you can comfortably walk with your two legs? You have awesome blessings!

~ It Is Well ~

1. You'll find the best disposition
Which provides you with thinking
Filled with great admonition
And prevents you from sinking.

2. Calming down and choosing a favourite
From all prevailing conditions
For that, I'll have the appetite
Not minding the other positions.

3. Your use of compliments
Good deeds you advocate
You cannot lack supplements
For which others salivate.

4. What crave for longevity
Defeats impending hunger?
As it turns your agility
And makes you younger.

5. Your display is quite mesmerising
As you perform so magically
Because of the way you're exercising
And making things move naturally.

Chapter 20
Disappointment Turned Into Blessing

Disappointment is the defeat of one's hope, and it can come up at any time in our lives. This feeling of dissatisfaction that follows the failure of expectations or hope to manifest, is a source of psychological stress, and can cause frustration and dejection in someone. The resultant effect may be depression. Disappointment, naturally, leaves us with unpleasant situations and bitter moments. It is a bitter pill to swallow, anyway. No one loves bitter pills the way people love chocolates, of course. No one would wish to be disappointed. It is an uninvited guest, so to say, but it comes, once in a while.

This phenomenon has ruined many individuals, families, career men & women, politicians, students, teachers, business men & women, suitors, wives, husbands, and so on. It is a very ugly word to meet, and a friend to none, but, it seeks friendship from all. There are disappointments and obstacles in everybody's life. No disappointment is unexpected - whether it is family life, career matters, academics, and so on. However, through disappointment, one can empower himself with the eventual discovery of what he would have positively done, earlier on, to achieve the desired success for his life.

'*Oh là là!*' That is the final expression, but initially, the expression was '*Ooohhh…!*' That is the fact in life. Without disappointments, or 'lows' of life, you cannot have testimonies of 'highs' of life. Without story, there is no history. Disappointment can turn into blessing when one approaches it with the right attitude.

Don't Be Carried Away By Emotions
Disappointment is never fun, anyway, but we should not be carried away by our emotions. Whether you are dealing with a relationship that has not worked out, or you have missed out on a major opportunity to advance your career, it is never as bad as it seems, and there are many more ways out than you may think. Just bear in mind that you are living in a world of 'second chance', because, disappointment will definitely pave in, giving you room for second chance,

and which you should tackle squarely.

You can deal with disappointment and come out stronger on the other side. After all, Helen Keller, (1880 - 1968), the blind and deaf woman who became a famous activist, and, who was for a time, the most famous handicapped person in the world, stated: "We would never learn to be brave and patient, if there were only joy in the world." Keller founded and promoted the American Foundation for the Blind. During her lifetime, she was regarded as one of America's most inspirational figures.

Some Cases Of Disappointment

Instances abound where people who were disappointed had to resort to self-destruction in forms of suicide, drug abuse, self-denial, and many other criminal tendencies. This redirection of thought does not, in any way, give room for positive thought which will unfold the person's blessings.

One lady had to drink poison because of being disappointed by a man who courted her for more than six years. She felt the rejection by that man was the end of her life. If she had accepted the fact that disappointment could come at any time, she would not have lived her life in such a way that, without that man, she would not survive. Did she know the better plan God had for her in terms of marriage? The fact that "if one door closes, another one opens," would have taught her a lesson. She ended up destroying her own life, because she felt disappointed. This, unfortunately, is a common practice, though they come in various forms.

The case of a man who went and hanged himself because he complained of seeking job for more than seven years without any headway, is still a bitter news. The man was not, in any way, handicapped; only that he was looking for a government job. As a matter of fact, he was very good in carpentry work, but he damned that, and put all his hope on the government work he was seeking. After the interview, he still had great hope of securing an appointment in that office. They kept on promising him that he would get the job, but, at the eleventh hour, he was informed that another man had been offered the job. A disappointment, anyway, but that was not supposed to terminate his life.

Dealing With Disappointments

One immediate thing you need to do as soon as you feel disappointed is to readjust your mindset. It is not a must that your wish will be carried out. One big factor that leads to disappointment is lack of patience. People are impatient; consequently, they feel let down at every opportunity. We need to fight this by adjusting our expectations. 'Rome was not built in a day,' is a popular saying, which is applicable here. How can you wish to be at the top when many others were there before you? So, people really need to adjust their expectations, in order not to feel disappointed.

Try not to be upset, to avoid health challenge. Take it that things can always be otherwise, and, in every bad situation, there are worse situations. I attended one funeral ceremony where a family lost one of the children. While consoling them, we felt pains for them. But surprisingly, the father of the child said: "We thank God, because, it would have been worse." I was surprised at that utterance for the loss of a child. As if the man read my mind, he went further to explain that it would have been worse if he had lost more than one child. So, the lesson here is that every bad condition would have been worse, but for the grace of God. So, we must learn to accept that we are better off.

For you to deal squarely with disappointments, you need to strain yourself to see silver lining. Rather than think that there is absolutely nothing positive in the situation, which is rarely the case, you need to find the good in the circumstance, to help you think positively. For instance, if you broke up with a person whom you thought was the love of your life, think deeply again to know if you were really so perfect for each other. If you lost your job, or did not get a particular job, ask yourself if it was really the best fit for you. Henry David Thoreau stated: "If we will be quiet and ready enough, we shall find compensation in every disappointment." Thoreau was an American author, naturalist, transcendentalist, tax resister, development critic, philosopher, and abolitionist. His philosophy of non-violent resistance influenced the political thoughts and actions of such later figures as Leo Tolstoy, Mohandas K. Gandhi, and Martin Luther King, Jr.

You can fight disappointment by being grateful for areas you have achieved. You will just find out that you do not need to feel marginalised, after all. When you lose a particular opportunity, you should consider your nice home, your intelligent children, your supportive parents, your good health, your promising career. When you stop thinking about the particular thing that went wrong, and start thinking about all the things that are going right in your life, then you will 'defeat disappointment'. Sure.

I quite agree with Conan O'Brien, an American television host, comedian, writer, producer, and voice actor, who stated: "the beauty is that, through disappointment, you can gain clarity, and with clarity comes conviction and true originality." When you encounter disappointment in life, do not rush into any action. Take some time to heal, so that you will let your feelings out, and acknowledge what has happened to you, to strategise on the way forward. A little bit of exercise, some music, some artistic expressions, can put you on the right track of recovery. You can start creating something beautiful.

As you take your time to reflect on what you can learn from your situation, do not ever blame yourself on the state of your affairs. You may, during the period of reflection, find out that your expectation was unrealistic, after all. Maybe, you do not have the exact qualification for that job you are seeking, or that you do not have enough money to buy that particular house you had all along hoped to own. Your time of reflection will give you the opportunity to think of what you can do better, in the future. We need to be encouraged by Thomas S. Monson, an American religious leader and author in his quote: "the principle of living greatly include the capacity to face trouble with courage, disappointment with cheerfulness, and trial with humility." This is a realistic approach to life challenges.

Disappointment Turned Into Blessing

At this point, we need to know that, sometimes, disappointment turns out to be blessing. When, on 22nd October 2005, Bellview Airlines Flight 210, a Boeing 737-200 aircraft, crashed at Lisa village, Ogun state, Nigeria, shortly after take-off from Murtala Muhammed International Airport in Lagos en route to the Nigeria capital, Abuja, killing all 117 people on board, the whole country was thrown into serious mourning mood. However, before the plane took off from Lagos, one man was desperate to follow that particular plane, but, he felt disappointed not to have gotten the chance, because he could not meet up with the flight departure time. He was still groaning at the airport for missing the flight, when, suddenly, the news filtered in, that the particular plane had crashed, with all the people on board dead! Can you still call this a disappointment for that man? No, of course. It has turned into a blessing for him. He had to go home to organise a special thanksgiving service in his church, to thank God for what he initially termed 'disappointment', but which metamorphosed into a blessing.

On another note, a girl was crying that she lost the love of her life, as the man left her to marry her own friend. But the law of nemesis usually catches up with such soul destroyers. It was a great disappointment to the girl, so, she reluctantly married another man. Today, that disappointment has turned into a blessing, because the husband is one of the forces to reckon with, in Nigeria today. Not only is he well-to-do, but he is such a caring and devoted husband. The man who initially met and disappointed her is now a mere drunkard and a nuisance to the society. The girl is ever grateful to God for that 'disappointment', now turned into blessing.

A student, for example, who fails an examination, needs to know that it is simply an opportunity for him to repeat, and concretise his knowledge. Sometimes, those who fail and repeat, come out with better stuff, as they are better exposed and equipped to face the challenges of the society. They become conscious of their actions, and consequently, perform greatly.

Sometimes, we feel that we are disappointed, when, in actual fact, our sweet blessings are hidden in shells coated with the bitter pills of disappointments. So, in every disappointment, lies something to thank God for. Difficulties come up so that one can appreciate the good things that one has. Disappointment is simply a delayed appointment. It will strengthen you, and will never destroy you.

Our Attitude Towards Disappointment

Since the world is full of pain, disappointments, and troubles, it behoves us to make it a better place to live in. Bearing in mind that a path with no obstacles leads nowhere, we have the ultimate choice of converting our difficulties into opportunities. Our attitude towards disappointing situation will be the determining factor of our turning point. Knowing well that the world is a hard place, we should embrace the idea that disappointment is a message that leads us to our destination of appointment.

Joseph Addison, an English essayist, poet, playwright, and politician, encouraged us thus: "Our real blessings often appear to us in the shape of pains, losses, and disappointments, but let us have patience, and we soon shall see them in their proper figures." What an admonition! This is a real counsel to those who feel deeply disappointed. Let us not be set back by the spirit of disappointments, because, if the great men and women we hail today were carried away by initial failures in their endeavours then, nothing would have been recorded in their honour. After all, what do Albert Einstein and Oprah Winfrey have in common? - They both faced early setbacks, but went on to do great things.

Today, Oprah Gail Winfrey (born in 1954), an American media proprietor, talk show host, actress, producer, and philanthropist, is best known for her multi-award winning talk show 'The Oprah Winfrey Show', which was the highest rated program of its kind in history, and was nationally syndicated from 1986 to 2011. She is dubbed the 'Queen of all Media', and has been ranked the richest African-American of the 20th Century, the greatest black philanthropist in American history, the first black woman billionaire in world history, and the most influential black person of her generation. All these came after her travails of early childhood - poverty, sexual abuse at age nine, teenage pregnancy, unmarried teenage mother who was a housemaid, molestations, and feelings of betrayal by family members.

Albert Einstein (1879-1955), told his biographer, Carl Seelig: "My parents were worried because I started to talk comparatively late, and they consulted a doctor because of it." Earlier on, in the recollections of the family recorded by Einstein's younger sister, Maja, in 1924, "Albert appears as calm, dreamy, slow, but self-assured and determined child." Today, we all know the story of Albert Einstein as the physicist who generated the world's most famous equation (Mass-Energy Equivalence $E = mc^2$).

Most times, success starts with disappointments. As Val Boyko, a leadership coach and career strategist working with individuals and organisations put it: "Life is a series of highs and lows. Be grateful for the highs. Be graceful in the lows. Enjoy life fully and find contentment in your Middle Ground." So, no one needs to take disappointment as the end of his life, rather, as a challenge, for such to turn to blessing.

~ **Blessing In Disguise** ~

1. In this our life of second chance
   There are many expectations
   Many things look fine at a first glance
   But we have to check the reflections.

2. In great shocks, treasures are hidden
   However, some are delayed
   In some cases, one is ridden
   But they'll surely be displayed.

3. In our utter disappointment
   We fail to work productively
   To get the desired appointment
   Which will come up surprisingly.

4. We have to remove the agitation
   Never allowing our lives to depreciate
   For us to get the compensation
   Which we'll definitely appreciate.

5. If we can just be thankful
   When certain problems arise
   We shall surely be graceful
   As blessings come in disguise.

Chapter 21
Show The Light

I t is always necessary to enlighten others. When we drive darkness, the resultant effect of illumination is witnessed, and this brings joy. It is by showing the light that our worth is brought to bear and the success of others is advocated. This equally leads to the full realisation of our being and the consequent self-empowerment. When I was appointed the Pioneer Principal of one of the Junior Secondary Schools in FCT, Abuja, I felt that it was a calling for me to go and 'show the light'. For clarification sake, that was the second Government school I was called to establish. Inspired by the biblical injunction which says: "Let your light so shine before men that they may see your good works, and glorify your Father which is in heaven," I was led to establish the school with the motto: 'Show The Light'.

My students were moved to appreciate that it was through their actions that the environment would be sanitised; their bright future would be guaranteed; and the nation would be exalted, as they were equally tutored that they were the salt of the nation. The regular recitation of the school motto by the students turned to be like an anthem, just as they equally sang the national and school anthems, so that no one would play ignorance of the motto of the school. I still feel proud of the staff and students who strived to live up to the motto of the school. Some of the students who have passed out from the school are testifying that they are really 'a light unto others' in their new places of abode and studies. This gives me joy and a sense of fulfilment.

This is a guiding principle, as I have lived to understand that, it is only in showing the light to others that we can also be established. Definitely, a tree cannot make a forest, which is why we must be led to showcase what we have, for others to imbibe, so that we can build a strong nation. If everyone should display what he or she is endowed with, without hoarding one's gifts, then the world would be a desirable place to live in.

A Little Recall
As a matter of recall, my very first posting as a principal of a secondary school in

FCT gave me a deep insight into what was expected of 'the leaders of tomorrow.' Realising that the bedrock of any nation lies greatly on the education of the children, I came up with the motto for that first school as: 'Education for Excellence'. Since I had the opportune time to be the very first principal of the school, I had to take a deep breath before coming up with that motto. That 'excellence' remains the watchword of the school till today. It is a great testimony that the pioneer head boy of that school gained admission to study Medicine in one of the Nigerian prestigious universities.

Of greater joy is the fact that some other products of that school have joined him in that course, while many others, who have really strived for excellence, are in other higher institutions and offering various courses. It is a pride to see that your products are doing well. They have worked with positive focus, seeing light at the end of the tunnel. These are the proverbial 'leaders of tomorrow', according to the wordings of their school anthem. These future leaders need the light to see the right footpaths to achieve their life ambitions. Time might not always give them the desires of their heart but as long as they stand firm, they will go to far greater heights.

Need For Light

We need to show the light wherever we find ourselves, because, as Martin Luther King Jr., the most important voice of the American civil rights movement, said, "Darkness cannot drive out darkness: only light can do that. Hate, cannot drive out hate: only love can do that." Martin Luther King Jr. worked for equal rights for all, and was famous for using non-violent resistance to overcome injustice. He also did all he could to make people realise that 'all men are created equal'.

There was a TV show sometime ago, where the blind people organised an event. Important dignitaries and government officials were invited, and the occasion was taking place in the night, so, everywhere was lit up. But something was wrong somewhere! The blind people were not seeing the beauty of the environment, the decorations made, and the things to be served. All of a sudden, as they were all about to eat, all the lights went off, and this lasted for about three minutes. All the invited guests started screaming, as they could not locate their food, the cutleries, their drinks, and other things provided for them.

The lights were left off for a few minutes, before the hall was illuminated once again. It was then that people heaved a sigh of relief. The purpose of the action was then explained — for the invited guests to understand what the blind ones were going through in life, not just for a few minutes, but

149 | Helen Uche Ibezim

throughout their life time, and consequently, to appreciate their own ability to see. This gives a perspective to how much we should appreciate the gift of our sight and work on spreading light to those in the dark.

The big question now is: 'are you showing light to others'?

Lead The Way

Selfishness is what mars us from showing the light. If you know the way, why don't you lead the others to victory? Cassandra Clare (born 1973), a notable American young adult fantasy novel writer, who earned numerous awards and prizes for her debut novel, *The City of Bones*, asserts thus: "whatever you are physically....male or female, strong or weak, ill or healthy - all those things matter less than what your heart contains. If you have the soul of a warrior, you are a warrior. All those other things, they are the glass that contains the lamp, but you are the light inside." True assertion indeed.

In your office, you can be a light unto others, when you assist them morally, financially, physically, and/or even emotionally. Your name will be written in gold, within their hearts. If you are in business, you may have a better strategy of 'doing it'. Why not show others the way? The people you assist today may be the ones to take care of your children tomorrow, according to H. Jackson Brown Jr, an American author best known for his inspirational book, *Life's Little Instruction Book*, which was a New York Times bestseller (1991-1994). This is because the best preparation for tomorrow is doing your best today.

Let us always be encouraged by gigantic strides made by some individuals, who are devotedly contributing to the economic growth of the nation today. The story of Sir Emeka Offor comes to mind at this point. He is an entrepreneur par excellence, and a philanthropist to the core. He has expansive business experience and has built a vast business with interests in many sectors of the economy. He sets big goals and enjoys the challenge of achieving the extraordinary. He believes in hard work and dedication to duties, and equally admires such qualities in others. He is focused, diligent, and courageous in his pursuit for excellence. He has a passion to uplift people and make them independent and self-sufficient.

In order to constantly render assistance to the needy in the society, irrespective of tribe and religion, he started the Sir Emeka Offor Foundation, as a vehicle for his philanthropic activities. The Foundation is committed to skills acquisition at the grassroots level; establishment of small and medium enterprises cooperative societies and small scale businesses; human and material capacity development. It has provided intervention programmes through Education Scholarship Scheme; Health Services Scheme; Youth Empowerment; Infrastructure Development Scheme; Widows Cooperative Scheme, and so on. Through all these services, the Foundation has been alleviating the suffering of the less privileged in the society, and has remained focused on giving support and hope to those in need. This is a realistic means of becoming powerful through one's gift. The lives touched will always appreciate such humanitarian ventures. Let us always be guided by the fact that it is left to one to make himself continuously relevant by maintaining one's own path of recognition in life.

Darkness Flees From Light

Darkness entails negativity in all aspects. It involves absence or deficiency of light; wickedness or evil; obscurity; concealment; lack of knowledge or enlightenment; lack of sight; blindness. Therefore, it is not possible for darkness and light to go together. Amit Ray, an Indian author and spiritual master, stated that when the sun of compassion arises, darkness evaporates and the singing birds come from nowhere. This goes to explain that when you have light, you are shielded from the negative traits of darkness.

A town or nation without education, for instance, is in darkness. A man that is displaying only wickedness to his fellow human beings is in darkness. A career person who is not thinking of advancing his career is in darkness. A community where people are perishing in ignorance is in darkness. So, darkness is a word that should not come close to light. He who brings light brings life, because, it is through light that one will be able to perceive life in its entirety.

We need to bring in light to drive away all those negative tendencies which are clothed within darkness. Imagine entering a room that is completely dark; you will be blind. But as soon as you switch on the bulb, or lighten the candle stick, you begin to see. Apart from our inner rooms, we also lighten the surroundings so that people with evil minds will be afraid of being caught, while trying to burst into the compound. It is true too that some night birds, like the owl, do not like light, so, they cannot come close to your lightened area. Where there is light, darkness must flee.

Lighten The World

You can lighten the world and make it a better place through your action of love, care, trust, loyalty, obedience, honesty, encouragement, and spirit of sportsmanship. The Nigerian election of 2015, for example, shall remain evergreen in the hearts of not only Nigerians, but also the hearts of the international community. The true show of love for peace, demonstrated by most Nigerians, through their conduct during and after the elections, kept the entire world dumbfounded. Contrary to expectations that there would be serious post-election violence or even serious war after the presidential election, the spirit of peace filled the air.

The full demonstration of the spirit of sportsmanship by the then serving President, Dr Goodluck Ebele Jonathan, in conceding defeat to Muhammadu Buhari, melted the hot atmosphere hanging in the air. What a lesson Jonathan taught the entire world! What a way to show the light to others! Honestly, it was a clear demonstration of paving way for peace. Consequently, he has become a hero - a man of distinguished courage and ability, admired for his brave deeds and noble qualities.

President Goodluck Jonathan exhibited an exalted moral and mental character of excellence, and became the first Nigerian presidential contestant that has called his rival to congratulate him. He ensured that he kept to his word, which has become one of the popular quotes, not only in Nigeria, but worldwide: "Neither my ambition, nor anybody's ambition, is worth the blood of any Nigerian." He has really shown the light to future presidential contestants, for them to clearly accept that, in any contest, a loser should accept the outcome, and support the winner. Indeed, he proved to the entire world that he is a true statesman - a person who is experienced in the art of government.

Professor Attahiru Jega, the Chairman of the Independent National Electoral Commission (INEC) during the period of 2015 Nigerian general elections, through his integrity, equally proved to be a man of honour. He showed great strength of character: focused, resilient, patient, wise, calm, cool, and calculated. Already his name is written in gold, in the history of this great country. Today, the whole world is hailing him for the courageous, intelligent, ingenious, and motivating way he carried out the election process in Nigeria. This great gentleman conducted the 2015 Nigerian general election which was adjudged by many, to be free, fair, and credible. This, he did, after conducting the 2011 general election, which was equally adjudged to be free and fair. In fact, Professor Jega has demonstrated a formidable election formula that the entire world would borrow and utilise in their various countries. As far as elections are concerned, the entire world would borrow a leaf from him, as he remains a competent resource person in that field.

Through strong team play which he carried out with his entire INEC staff, the spirit of loyalty, obedience, and trust, came to bear. The introduction of the wonderful smart card reader which gave authenticity to each voter, and transparency in the process, is a revolutionary innovation, which the present and the future generations in this country will ever cherish. Through the support of the devoted members of staff and the entire ingenious directors of the commission, he was able to come up with gargantuan ideas, which have proved fruitful in the election process.

What I see in INEC is a strong team work, and a sense of dedication to duty. It is worthy of note that, the directors, through their various departments, have shown the light to the nation, and generations yet unborn. The ingenuity of the ICT department, for instance, in ensuring that the card readers were valuable tools during the last election in the country, motivated the electorate to turn out in great numbers. Through that, much confidence was built in the voters, as each voter went through that accreditation process with no doubts of authentication. Bravo! That is a way of making the light to shine. Truly, they have shown the light and the citizens are proud of such genuine ventures.

Apart from exhibiting a spirit of sportsmanship, you can still lighten the world through your action of loyalty. No man is an island. Human beings are bound to offer one form of assistance or the other to fellow human beings, for progress to be recorded. In the case of any administration, a good citizen shows the light to others through his sense of being firm in allegiance to the government. When you give your support, things will work out better. In the words of Tommy Lasorda, regarded by many as baseball's most popular Ambassador: "You give loyalty, you'll get it back. You give love, you'll get it back."

Try to encourage people. When you see that people are making efforts, encourage them, so that they can beef up efforts. Encouragement is a way of recognising the good others do, and, applauding their success. You should not just be a fault finder, but seek ways of applauding the right things in people, so that they will strive to do better. Always show gratitude to people when they are the ones who do something for you.

Always show love. If you love someone, you will not like to display dishonesty; rather, you will always be transparent in your dealings with others. Since love is the most important virtue, you can always succeed when you equip yourself with this tool. Through love, your show of care for others will be manifested, your obedience to the rule of law will be upheld, and your disposition in all facets of life will not be questionable. If you demonstrate your ability to show love, you will be surprised at how good things will keep on unfolding for you. Sow righteousness and reap the fruit of unfailing love. Make the world sweeter through your sweet love. By making the world a better place, the light in you will be beaming. You will be like the city on a hilltop that cannot be hidden.

Life Of Empowerment

By showing light to somebody, you can empower that person for life. You can think of a situation where somebody is always looking for a piece of fish to eat each day. Someone from somewhere may suddenly emerge to show that person the way to fish. He is definitely showing the light to that person and consequently, empowering him with the way to catch fish and eat on a daily basis. It will be quite an exciting experience for the person being empowered. The saying that we should not just give a fish to a hungry man, but that we should teach him how to fish, is really appreciated here.

Place yourself in a position to teach others how to control their circumstances and achieve their own goals in life. You can equip somebody with internet facilities to enable that person make his own research on how to better his lifestyle and career. You can equally buy books on relevant issues in life, and give someone as gifts. Through that means, the recipient will be able to wriggle out of his worrisome situation. You can decide to pick some children from your community, if you are kind and buoyant enough to do that, by showing them the light of life, through scholarships and continuous mentoring. At the end of the training, they are surely empowered.

Some people do not realise that when they are getting weak in service, it is the ones they empowered that will assist them in old age. You will be surprised at the kind of assistance they will be rendering to you because, as an Igbo proverb says: "It is the firewood you gather during the dry season that you will use during the rainy season when you can no longer get dry ones." Live a life of empowering people, because your own life will become more meaningful through that practice.

A Golden Fish Has No Hiding Place

We can witness the apt comparison of the power of good deeds in William Shakespeare's The Merchant of Venice. This is made more prominent through Portia's speech, when she puts words to her admiration of the candlelit beauty of an estate. She proclaims: "How far that little candle throws his beams! So shines a good deed in a naughty world."

A good deed can never be overlooked, just as a golden fish has no hiding place, because of its captivating nature. A goldfish is beautiful, peaceful, and mesmerising. In same way, a person with good deeds is always captivating, because of the light radiating in him. I remember one man, Corporal Solomon Dauda, a traffic warden in Abuja, who was conferred with a National Award in

2014 by President Goodluck Jonathan, because of his demonstration of great dexterity, glee, and content in the duty he was performing. Commuters were taking note of his unique way of controlling the traffic as he danced and exhibited some forms of gesticulations while efficiently directing traffic. His graceful gyrations were not only entertaining but demonstrating satisfaction with his job. He performed his duty with passion, evident pride and dignity. Little did he know that his manner of approach to his job would earn him a National Award! Surprisingly, he was rewarded with an award of 'Member of Order of the Niger' and a house.

The National Honours Award, which is an annual event, (established by the National Honours Act of 1964), empowers the President by warrant to use the Nigerian Order of Dignity to honour deserving citizens who have contributed to the development and progress of the country in any field of human endeavour. It is conferred on men and women of proven integrity for their hard work, diligence, honesty and dedication to duty. Solomon Dauda, through his performances, has consequently shown the light, and his colleagues are thereafter motivated to work assiduously like he has done. Just do your good deeds. Whatever you are gifted with, make it your power, for others to benefit from you. Your gift remains your possession, but, it is left to you to make it a powerful instrument for use.

~ Let My Light Shine ~

1. For me to show the light
I'll fight with all my might
Even if it means leaving my comfort zone
I will shine, rather than in darkness groan.

2. Oh! I shall keep this candle
To throw the light to everyone
I shall never hide it
But ensure the world becomes far brighter

3. Striving for that excellence
Will demand all my patience
In order for me to admire
My heart - long desire.

4. How awesome it will be
For me to learn to be free
As light shines on my face
I will receive His grace.

5. My light of life will shine
And I will surely dine
In such a glorious way
To keep the devil at bay.

Chapter 22

Be On Guard!

This is a state of being vigilant; being watchful, keeping safe from harm or danger; and being careful to avoid being tricked or getting into a dangerous situation. Being on guard means that, in your thoughts, 'anything can happen'. Of course, no one can predict what will happen in the next moment; hence precautionary measures are very important in our lives. If we are not cautious in our actions, unlocking our potentials will be threatened.

Who Do You Associate With?

You need to be mindful of whom to trust these days. Some people are so overconfident in others that they 'sell' off themselves to such treacherous ones. Trust is expensive and should not be offered easily. It should be earned.

Check your associates very well. Do not just cling on to someone simply because you want to establish a relationship. Your personality is mostly measured by the kind of friends you keep; which goes to say you should not even trust your presence in the company of some people before you get the tag of being like them. This is what informs the saying: 'Show me your friend and I will tell you who are.' Take time to find out the true lifestyle, principles and worldview of anyone you are associating with. The days are evil, so you need to protect your life.

Check On Your Children

Frank Olize, a former NTA veteran broadcaster and presenter always started the popular Sunday NTA magazine programme, Newsline saying: "Do you know where your children are?" This remains a vital question. This question used to move many parents to start calling their children to know their dispositions at that particular point in time. A consistent check on your children makes them know you care and that you can check on them at any time. This keeps them on their guard and away from doing the constant evil they otherwise might have tried. They always await your call. Consequently, they adjust and reduce negative tendencies. A parent who ignores the protection of his children is not worthy to be called a parent.

Constant check on your children shows that you are proactive. They are your jewels of inestimable value, so you would naturally not love to lose them. That is a way of showing them love and care. Monitoring their school activities, to prevent a situation of being dismissed from school, is necessary. Their academic records should be on your fingertips, to know when they are progressing and when they are, possibly, retrogressing. This is to know when to assist them, especially during preparations for exams.

Apart from their academics, their moral disposition should be closely monitored by you. You should be on guard always, as far as these children are concerned. Help them avoid a life of regret, by averting ugly and embarrassing situations. When you know the kind of friends your children keep, and these friends are the right kind, your mind will be at rest when they go on visits. Encourage them to bring their friends to the house so that you can advise them on proper lifestyles, especially while away.

Being on guard is not the sole responsibility of parents, because, children leave their homes to go to different places particularly school. School administrators and teachers who are always glued to the chairs in their offices will not be able to have proper checks on the students. You must develop the eyes of an owl —looking in all directions —to control the children under your care. It is possible for you to be luxuriating inside your office, while the students are busy burning down a classroom, or killing one another with dangerous weapons. You need to sit up, if you must achieve the goal of administration.

In every aspect of life, close monitoring should be used where children are concerned. Parents should endeavour to provide the needs — not really the wants — of the children, to reduce the tendency of the children seeking assistance through immoral means. An example is in the handling of the girl-child. She is tender and consequently, becomes possible prey to those dangerous men who will never allow anything in skirt to pass them by. When your girl-child has her basic needs met, she will find it difficult to follow those immoral men. This is also applicable to the boy-child who may have the tendency of being lured into unacceptable behaviours, like robbery and kidnapping, to get money.

Obeying The Rules

Every action has a guiding principle. There are rules governing various activities. Driving, for instance, requires a driving licence. To be in accordance with the law, those who are driving are expected to have their drivers' licences. A driving licence is a privilege that can be revoked under certain conditions including road misdemeanours. Consequently, driving without a valid driver's licence attracts serious consequences. It is illegal, and should not be practised. Knowing fully well that you may be asked to pay a fine, or even have your vehicle impounded if you flout this order demands that you should not go against this law.

A person's driver's licence is usually the most important thing in your wallet. It identifies you as a licensed driver. Without it, you have no right to operate a vehicle on public roadways. It serves as one's official personal ID, as it displays your contact information and a picture that officials can compare to the person who is presenting it as identification. It allows emergency officials to identify you if you are involved in an accident, as the name and address will help them locate and contact family members to inform them of your injuries. The information on the licence equally enables hospital staff to begin the admission process, when necessary. Since this document is so valuable, you have to be very careful in handling it. You need to take proper care not to lose it. Importantly too, you have to use it always. That is the law.

Some people drive vehicles without the vehicle particulars, which include the vehicle insurance certificate, and road worthiness certificate. Carrying the vehicle particulars with you is just to prove that you are the legitimate owner of the vehicle you are carrying. This is an evidence of proper and genuine documentation of such vehicle. This check makes it easier to arrest thieves who have carted away other people's vehicles. When offenders fall into the hands of traffic officials, they develop 'sudden fever', because of the consequences.

In addition to having your documents, obeying the traffic rules is another important civic responsibility. These rules include: obeying traffic signs; buckling of seat belts; avoiding over-speeding, phone calls while driving, drunk-driving, under-aged driving, and so on. You should always think of every possible occurrence when you are driving. You are simply being proactive, and getting yourself set for any eventuality. You are applying preventive measure, rather than curative approach. As the popular saying goes: it is better to be safe than sorry; prevention is better than cure.

It is not only on roads that we have rules to obey; this is also applicable to the school system, in the offices, and in various organisations. Knowing well that constant absenteeism from work, for instance, may lead to your sack, you can avoid that sack by making your presence and services available most times. The instruction that school rules and regulations must be obeyed to avoid being suspended from school, will give room to the students to adhere strictly to the regulations of the school, to avoid the embarrassment of being suspended, or even expelled from the school. The expression of 'Once beaten, twice shy', should move us into being on guard always. It is true that 'experience is the best teacher', but we should not wait to have an ugly experience before we can learn, as we can equally learn from the experience of others.

Be Cautious

In our various homes, we have many gadgets. We should have a feeling that any of such things could be destroyed by fire at any time. This is why we need fire extinguishers in our homes. The use of gas cooker, for example, is common these days, but, we need to play safe in the use of such. It is not advisable to place the gas cylinder inside the kitchen, but, outside, because of possible fire outbreak.

On another note, there are those who are not cautious about divulging information entrusted in their care. Some government workers are so loose that they disclose official secrets which some tricksters use to work against the government. The guiding principle of oath of secrecy is supposed to guard against such. However, many of them ignore this. For the work to be sanitised, we need to guard our mouths. Watching our utterances is a must.

The need to be cautious while walking or moving around is equally necessary. Some of the people you meet at some places like markets, parks, churches, and mosques, did not really go there for genuine reasons. Some are mere opportunists looking for the least possible way to extort your items. There are recorded cases where vehicles were stolen from church premises and mosques. You need to find better and safer ways of protecting your belongings. Endeavour to lock all doors before going to bed.

Precautionary measures should always be taken. I saw a car parked on a highway some time ago. Unfortunately, a lorry on a high speed just ran into it, thereby scattering the parts because, there was no notification or warning sign to the oncoming vehicle that the car was not on motion. One wonders if such an accident might have happened if the driver had been cautious enough to put leaves or some other signs to show that there was a stationary car there.

Mind Your Security Status

This is all about being aware of your safety status and how to handle eventualities. The places one is prone to threat, risk, and dangers are: at home, at work, at school, at market places, at parks, at gardens, and, even on transit. We are in a period of uncertainties, with many evil-minded people operating at all nooks and corners, instilling the negative feelings of fear and anxiety in innocent people's minds. There are terrorists, armed robbers, assassins, kidnappers, fraudsters of various degrees, operating here and there. This trend therefore calls for measures to curb these occurrences which are ravaging the society.

It is always advisable to walk in company of someone, rather than walking alone, especially during odd hours. This will, to a reasonable extent, reduce the risk of falling into evil people's hands. Even if anything happens, someone will be able to inform your family members what must have happened.

Being secretive is necessary when you are with strangers. Do not share your personal information with strangers, because the enemy intercepts such information to perpetrate crime. You should be using randomness in your daily operations, so that those trailing you will not predict what you will do at any point in time. Avoid following the same route all the time. Avoid using same ATM password for a long time. When you allow some form of randomness in your life, it will be difficult for the enemy to strike. Talk less. Be very observant. Observe everything - your car, the public bus, your compound, your gardens, and so on. Try to be as simple as possible, and avoid unnecessary show of wealth, because, that may sometimes attract the envy of some enemies. When we are aware that some people are sadists, we reduce the rate of displaying what we have, for example, flashy cars, expensive phones, gold, diamond, and platinum jewelleries. Sometimes, these things pose as threats to your life.

Always be informed about the current happenings in your environment. Listening to the daily news on radio and television, in addition to reading newspapers, will equip you with valuable information on the state of affairs in your country or state. Remain informed. Any suspicious movement around your area of abode should be reported to the police. Interrogate people whose identities are unknown to you, so that you will be sure that those people are genuinely operating there.

Avoid Being Deceived

Deception is an occurrence in every sphere of life. In the school, for instance, some students go into a hideout for their private studies, but later surface to deceive others who may wish to study. Beware of such. You may find yourself playing with them during exams, but later, you see them emerging successful after exams, while you fail.

In the office, some staff pay lip service to the Chief Executives, thereby giving room to overconfidence on the part of the administrator. This leads to complacency in the administrative style, with consequential low output. We should be mindful of such insincere people. Along the streets, there are instances of innocent citizens being tricked into releasing their money to fraudsters. Many have been duped already. The unassuming approach used by these cheats leaves the victims hopeless.

We need to be careful, to avoid being tricked or pushed into dangerous situations. There is a funny story told of a teacher who was invigilating an examination. He observed that two students were discussing in the exam hall. Furiously, he went straight to them and asked: "What are you doing?" They cleverly answered: "We are discussing, because, the question says 'Discuss the importance of Agriculture'." It took the intelligence of the teacher to dissuade them from the meaning the students attached to the question. If he was not clever, those students would have put him into trouble of 'aiding and abetting', during exams. So, beware of deceptive, uncertain, and tricky people around you.

Value Your Time And Spare Moments

If you have spare moments, be conscious of the fact that they have to be used optimally. Ralph Waldo Emerson, an American poet, lecturer, and essayist, advises thus: "Guard well your spare moments. They are like uncut diamonds. Discard them and their values will never be known. Improve them and they will become the brightest gems in a useful life." Do not use your spare moments to gossip, to commit character assassination, or to look for ways of pulling others down. Think of how to make your life a better one.

Being Proactive

This is a situation of tending actively to instigate changes, in anticipation of future developments, as opposed to merely reacting to events as they occur. Octavia Spencer, an American film actress and television actress, skilled in both comedy and drama, stated that the way to bring about change is to be proactive and active. Of course, being proactive means being reactive ahead of time.

You are proactive, when you think and act ahead of anticipated events. That means you have foresight. This, when applied, helps reduce a lot of disasters that could happen. It is the proactive people that instigate actions and create ideas in the society. For you to avert ugly situations, you need to reflect on the actions that may come up, and how to give them attention when they come. You then go ahead to plan, think critically how to carry those tasks efficiently, through creation of plan and checklist. When you make plans, it is always advisable to equally make an alternative plan, in case the first one fails. That is what we popularly call 'Plan B'. You can even go ahead to have 'Plan C', just to make sure that the required action is taken up. Find out which actions can come up before the others - prioritising your actions is very important.

The foresight you have, through your trait of being proactive, will save you from a lot of embarrassments. For instance, if you are using electricity powered through the prepaid meter reading, you do not have to wait until the credit gets exhausted, before you reload. Definitely, you will put yourself in embarrassing situation. You can imagine your house being in darkness, when all your neighbours' houses are lit. However, a proactive person will always ensure that he does not wait for the credit to exhaust, so that he will not put himself in a stressful situation.

The use of cooking gas is another area for someone to display proactive nature. A standby filled up gas cylinder will make you not to run helter-skelter when the one you are currently using gets finished. It gives you time to get yourself relaxed when emergency situation comes up. You do not need to stress your brain, rushing to look for where to get gas, to complete what you are cooking, because you have been proactive enough to keep a standby filled gas cylinder for immediate replacement of the empty one.

It is a common occurrence these days to see some cars ignite, due to lack of necessary checks before the drivers took off. In the event of such, some control measures would equally have taken place if the cars were equipped with the required fire extinguishers. Unfortunately, some drivers just pick the car keys in the morning, and zoom off, without checking the engine oil, the quantity of fuel in the car, the brake fluid, the tyres, and some other necessary parts. But gladly, some conscious drivers do not take off until all the routine checks have been performed, thus, moving out with higher confidence of performance by the vehicles. The case of fire outburst will not be a big problem if that comes up at all, because the fire extinguisher is already there in the vehicle, to perform its task.

Executives of various offices and organisations should be on guard to know when members of their staff are demoralised. Check their dispositions constantly, and find out if they are planning an industrial action, so that you can appease them by looking critically into their grievances. After all, without such staff, you cannot operate optimally. Seek ways of getting things done in a rather precautionary way, than when damages have already occurred.

All That Glitters Is Not Gold

It is not everything that is shiny and attractive that is valuable. It is not everything that looks precious that turns out to be real. This is applicable to people, places, or things, that promise to be more than what they really are. Judging people on the basis of mere appearance can be greatly misleading. A person may be good-looking but may be very wicked and mean. On the contrary, there are some people whose looks are not so attractive, but have hearts of gold.

Beware of fake people in your life. A fake person is someone who is not genuine and will do whatever it takes to make himself look good. He takes credit for other's work and downplays the good of others to illuminate himself. He takes part in hypocrisy, lies, and will quit friendship the moment it is not beneficial to him. He changes his personality to fit in to a certain group. You can easily detect a fake person through the way he deals with your ups and downs. When you are feeling down, your fake friend will merely pat you awkwardly on the shoulder and try to change the subject, rather than wrap you in his arms to listen to your complaints as a real friend should.

Real friends are reliable. They will always be with you through thick and thin, but fake friends will leave you at the least of challenges. Their smiles have always been to either get things from you or for you to favour them, but as soon as a little problem crops up, they will flee from you. They will not even identify with you as close friends. They are terrible.

Fake friends can only blossom with you when you are doing greatly, but, a little mistake can cost your friendship, unlike the real friend, who will forgive you and value your friendship more than your temporary mistake.

Fake people can be as dangerous as snakes. They only seek to betray you through their fake smiles, backhanded compliments, talk behind your back and even the mockery they make of you. They are the ones who will initiate your downfall and still come back to sympathise with you. They 'accompany the spirit to kill and turn around to condole'. They are horrible people and should not be associated with. A fake person can only dress to impress. Do not be tempted to be attracted by that. He may have borrowed the dress or he may have stolen it. That is mere aesthetic display. What of the inner mind? What is the intention of that person coming close to you? Be careful.

Without wisdom, we cannot really undertake such precautions. "The only true wisdom," according to Socrates, "is in knowing you know nothing." Socrates was the most famous philosopher of classical Greece. He was an Athenian citizen, who revolutionised the way people thought about themselves and the world, and was famous for his questioning teaching method - Socratic Method. Through Socrates' assertion, you will always strive to get the knowledge on what to do, in every challenging situation. Be on guard, always.

~ Fasten Your Seat Belt ~

1. Something will surely happen
And your spirit may likely dampen
Be on guard
And prepare to play life a card...

2. For every spare moment
You have to make it potent
If you're always on check
You will avoid life's wreck.

3. A life of randomness
Will yield you happiness
You have to flee from obscurity
For you to get your security.

4. When you don't play the caution
You are opting for auction
Some people are treacherous
And their actions are dangerous.

5. If you don't have a weapon
It means you're with mere melon
Beware of all that glitters
Not all that truly matters.

Chapter 23

Self-Discipline

This is the ability to control one's feelings and overcome one's weaknesses. It is the training of oneself and one's conduct, usually for personal improvement. This is a great virtue for the successful growth of someone, especially, in the area of one's empowerment with his talents. It is one thing to know what is right, and another thing to do it. This exercise of self-discipline plays a vital role in our lives. It promotes the level of your acceptability in the society.

Right-minded persons prefer to associate with self-disciplined people. Though it is the hard path of life, the truth needs to be told; no matter how bitter. One who desires self-discipline should be ready to act in opposition to his natural desires and inclinations. Self-denial is his way of life; because, he will surely find himself not doing what he would ordinarily like to do, due to prudence or conscience. However, this is a rewarding virtue.

Some Instances Of Self-discipline

There are various ways we can exercise self-discipline. Some concrete instances are mentioned below:

- Refraining from lies -Wow! Some people cannot survive without telling lies. Everything about them is just fallacy. You are expected to stand on, and for, the truth, no matter the circumstance. It is said that the truth shall set us free. This is a very serious area of self-discipline.
- Bringing yourself down, for the interest of others, when it is natural for you to raise yourself up - Due to the proud nature of some persons, they hardly accept to humble themselves, to see the goodness in others.
- Accepting to do a work that is supposed to be done, even when you are not willing to do that- It is not always that you get exactly what you want. Some tasks are acting as challenging agents to you, so you need to be up.
- Refraining from nagging or grudges, even when situations seem unpleasant to you- Note, if you are known for this, you will constitute

a nuisance to people staying with or around you.

- Refusing to accept bribe even when your pocket is dry- Some people, due to the hardship they experience, live a life of bribery and corruption. This is not a good resort.

- Waking up early in the morning to carry out your normal responsibilities in order to 'catch the train'- It is the discipline that will make you not luxuriate on bed, when you are supposed to be engaged in one useful activity or the other.

- Refraining from eating too much or eating what has been prohibited for you to eat- Some people are gluttons. Table etiquette has no place in their lives, at all. It is you who will bring yourself to terms with just what your body requires.

- Refraining from drinking alcohol, even when you love it so much!- If someone else can survive without it, why can't you, especially when you have been warned by your doctor? Do not drink because others are drinking; caution your lifestyle to obey your needs, not your wants.

- Denying yourself sexual pleasures before marriage-There is time for everything, so do not be in a hurry to go into that, because of the consequences. You may be unlucky to contact some sexually transmitted diseases; you may be unlucky to be put in the family way (in case of girls); or to be forced to marry someone, when you are not yet ready for that (in case of boys). There are many negative results from this practice.

- Abstaining from extra-marital affairs, for those who are already married -Infidelity can cost you your life because of the extent some spouses can go to avenge such ugly trait. The picture of a man who claimed to be a man of God was once posted on the Facebook, with the woman he was caught committing adultery with (both naked). It was a very ugly situation and an unpleasant sight. As a teacher, for instance, you may be tempted into luring a female student to sexual immorality, but STOP! When you avert the seduction, you will see how happy you will be with yourself. If you do not respect your heart's inner warning, you will have a life of regrets. Nothing is hidden under the sun, you know.

- Refusing to follow other members of staff in running an organisation down, through lateness, truancy, squandering of funds, and so on- No matter how you feel about your place of work, you were placed there to build, never to destroy. Be a builder, not a destroyer.

- Refusing to follow other students to join cultist groups, even when you feel insecure in the school- Some students, out of eagerness to 'belong' to the 'powers of destruction', leave themselves to fall into the trap of these destiny destroyers.
- Pulling yourself out from the crowd to go and have your private study- This is a powerful decision, as you can as well, have many other interesting things happening around you, which you may gladly wish to do, like watching the TV or lying down on your bed.
- Not allowing yourself to watch pornographic films, pictures, or videos- Others may lure you into venturing to know what is obtainable there, but you are the one to discipline yourself in abstaining from such practice.

Commit To Self-discipline Now!

Committing to self-discipline requires that you have to avoid procrastination and distractions. Constant making of proposals, without carrying them out, is as nonsensical as not proposing them at all. If you pronounce that you wish to stop smoking, for example, get involved immediately, by refusing to send anybody to buy cigarettes for you. You can equally distance yourself from those selling such.

The practice of declaring: "I'll stop it next week" or "I'll stop it when I get married," is not a good habit. Some will keep on postponing their studies until the exam period. Some will say that they will start putting to practice their inborn talents only when they grow up. These procrastinations will never help you unravel what is in you. If you really want to be guided by self-discipline, you have to be action-oriented. You must be forward-looking to achieving what you have in mind, so that you will be moved by such passion.

Committing to self-discipline is not an easy task; therefore, your persistence in maintaining your focus is required. Set yourself back on track as often as possible. Repetition and continuous practice are necessary ingredients for your self-discipline. A situation whereby you make your sporting activities regular, for instance, sets you in the right frame of mind.

Without a plan, you may not go far in any meaningful venture. So, for you to successfully commit to self-discipline, you have to clearly define the goals that you want to attain. This will serve as a guide to you reaching the top of the ladder. You have to be ready to accept responsibility, and note that you are the one controlling your direction in life. Build up a positive state of mind. This is a sure way to maintain self-discipline.

Perseverance Is Worthy

Perseverance simply means doing something continuously, despite difficulty, in the hope of achieving success. Sometimes, we wish to record some achievement, but there are hitches here and there. In the school system, for instance, a child may often find himself failing exams. Some persons may equally experience some setbacks in trying to achieve a particular goal. This is where perseverance comes into play. When you find yourself in a challenging situation, and you need to exhibit self-discipline, you have to imbibe the spirit of perseverance, in order to succeed. You have to maintain a purpose, in spite of difficulty.

For every worthy venture in life, especially in the unlocking of one's potential, perseverance is noteworthy. I buy the idea of Maya Angelou who stated: "You may encounter many defeats, but you must not be defeated. In fact, it may be necessary to encounter the defeats, so you can know who you are, what you can rise from, how you can still come out of it." Maya Angelou (1928 - 2014), was an African-American author, poet, playwright, director, stage and screen performer. Equally, Confucius, whose philosophy emphasised personal and governmental morality, correctness of social relationships, justice and sincerity, stated: "It does not matter how slowly you go, as long as you do not stop."

I was at the stadium where some sports men and women were jogging in a mock race. Some started with much enthusiasm and rush, but they could not finish the race. Some started with others, though not in a hasty way, but, got tired in the course of the race. Some of them chose not to continue, but I noticed one man who persevered, and reached the finishing point. A prize was given to him afterwards. He was determined to reach there, so, he imbibed the spirit of perseverance, to be able to attain his goal of success. This gives an idea of perseverance and determination in this race of life.

Anyone who has experienced mountain climbing, for instance, will surely appreciate what it means to persevere. My personal experience in climbing Mount Sinai in Egypt, when I went on Christian Pilgrimage, was a true test of perseverance. My ability to reach the peak of the mountain, with some other pilgrims, gave me great joy and a sense of fulfilment. But this was not without some stops here and there, as a result of fatigue. However, the more I felt tired, the more I felt the need to 'finish the race', especially when I saw some of the pilgrims descending from the mountain top. It was a very tight decision for me, because of the pains I started experiencing, but I was determined! At last, I made it!!!

Perseverance makes you not to moan or cry when tough or negative situations crop up, as you will be able to absorb them and keep a positive attitude. This virtue needs to be instilled in children who are going to school, so that they will be encouraged and challenged when going through difficult times at school, or with their friends. It equally needs to be imbibed by those seeking appointments, so that they will realise that genuine positions cannot be gotten through crude or foul means.

There is no doubt that those who persevere make better managers. In world history today, all great men and women, inventors, popular athletes, successful business men and women, made it through perseverance. This virtue often determines the winners and also the losers. Those people who have made great marks would have had success elude them if they had not gone that 'one extra step'. Worthy of mention is Abraham Lincoln of the United States of America. He was faced with defeat most of his life. He lost eight elections, failed twice in business and suffered a nervous breakdown.

Lincoln recorded many failures and setbacks, starting from his birth into a very poor family, in 1809, in a one-room log cabin on Nolin Creek in Kentucky. In 1818, young Abe Lincoln, as he was also known, was kicked in the head by a horse, and, for a brief moment, was thought to be dead. That same year, his mother died of 'milk sickness'. He did not let this deter him but took courage to soar in various life pursuits. Lincoln's political career was filled with few 'highs' and many 'lows'. In 1832, he ran for state legislature, and lost. Though he ran for state legislature again in 1834 and won, he sought to become Speaker of the state legislature in 1838, but was defeated. In 1840, he sought to become elector (a member of the Electoral College in the U.S.), but was defeated. Once again, he lost, when he ran for Congress in 1843. After running for Congress again in 1846 and winning, he ran for re-election to Congress in 1848 and lost. Later on, in 1854, he ran for Senate of the United States, and lost. When he sought the Vice-Presidential nomination at his party's national convention in 1856, he got less than one hundred votes. Furthermore, he had to run for U.S. Senate again in 1858, but lost again!!! All these attempts and failures did not deter him from trying further. With the spirit of determination to succeed, he was finally elected President of the United States in 1860. What a journey! Lincoln was indeed a champion.

Note that he did not quit. He continued pursuing his dream and eventually won the seat of the President of the United States of America (1861-1865). Not only that, he went ahead to become one of the greatest presidents in the history of America.

Relatively in Nigeria is the story of President Muhammadu Buhari. As a General, he was Nigeria's Head of State from 31st December 1983 to 27th

August 1985. Within that time, along with his second-in-command, General Tunde Idiagbon, he started the famous anti-corruption and discipline campaign tagged 'War Against Indiscipline' (WAI). It helped to bring about a reorientation in the manners of Nigerians and brought a more positive image of the country in the international community. General Buhari was ousted from office by General Ibrahim Badamasi Babangida. After experiments that failed, democracy returned to Nigeria in 1999.

Buhari felt that he still had some greater plans for the nation that he could put to effect in the new democratic dispensation. He waited the first tenure to pass and then joined the Presidential race in 2003. This goal, he pursued, with full determination and vigour. He persevered. He lost the elections in 2003 to President Olusegun Obasanjo. In 2007, he lost to Umaru Yar'adua. In 2011, he lost the Presidential elections to Goodluck Ebele Jonathan. Despite all the setbacks, he did not give up, but rather, geared up, joining forces with many great men. He put aside every past disgrace and loss, contested against President Goodluck Ebele Jonathan for the second time in 2015 and won, becoming the first opposition presidential candidate to defeat an incumbent in Nigeria. At last, he was able to make it to Aso Rock, becoming the fifth democratically elected President of the Federal Republic of Nigeria. His demonstration of self-discipline is capped in his inaugural speech when he declared "I belong to everybody and I belong to nobody," meaning that he was ready to work with everyone, irrespective of tribe, religion, or political affiliation.

Setting One On The Right Track

Self-discipline, be it in children or in adults, when achieved, manifests in a number of rewarding ways. It helps one fulfil promises he makes to himself and to others. Without restraints, people are ready to be talking like parrots, promising to build castle in the air, for others. But with this attribute, one already has a check on himself, so that he will be properly guided.

In the case of children, a self–disciplined child in the classroom will achieve easier learning. It is through self-discipline that a child will ignore group pressure. No matter what the group is doing, the child will single himself out. He will complete his assignments. This is as a result of being set on the right track by self-discipline. Of course, teachers are at their best when children do their assignments. That is evidence that they are following the lesson. A self-disciplined child chooses productive, rather than destructive activities. You can never see such a child where others are fighting or bullying, but you will see him where activities like debates, drama, quiz, are going on.

Control of tempers by both children and adults is as a result of self-discipline. It is due to self-discipline that one does not act rashly and on impulse. One will think before he acts. He will look before he leaps. If we allow ourselves to be carried away by our temperaments, then, someone may be ready to burn a house! Restraint is the watchword. Due to restraint in the eating habit of some people, they have been able to maintain their desired shapes and healthy status. This virtue is good for the system to explore and execute its laid down rules and regulations.

Overcoming the habit of spending too much time on films and videos is through this special virtue. One will definitely be pushed to ask himself why he is wasting so much time on the TV set. You are moved to go to the gym for some sporting activities due to discipline that forms a new way of life. Ordinarily, you may decide to waste your time on useless talks with people who do not have vision in life.

Self-discipline imbibes the spirit of accomplishing set projects which pushes procrastination away. You would not want your efforts to be in vain, even after you may not feel so interested in that again. It makes you overcome laziness and procrastination. Nothing causes lack of production, like laziness. Self-discipline defeats this practice and sets you on the track again.

Happy Moments

Self-discipline seems to be dreary at times but the end result is juicy. Remember the saying: "the harder the fight, the sweeter the victory." Self-discipline is an avenue for someone to have the ability to achieve that which he really needs, to succeed in life. It is taxing though, but nothing good comes easy. It does not just end with self-denial, neither does it earn instant gratification, but it comes with a very big reward at the end, and that is long-term contentment.

Guru Gobind Singh, a spiritual master, warrior, poet, and philosopher, observed thus: "Peace and happiness shall fill your mind deep within, if you act according to truth and self-discipline." Stop thinking that self-discipline is deprivation of pleasures and happiness. People with self-discipline are happier, because they avoid situations that may create problematic desires and conflict; consequently, they experience fewer negative emotions. We all need to imbibe the spirit of self-discipline in order to earn ourselves happy moments and success that we all crave for.

~ **Up And Out** ~

1. Getting up and trying to venture,
Equipped with full perseverance
To move on with my desired adventure
And make a worthwhile appearance.

2. To great deeds I will commit
Gathering all the materials
Ensuring that I'll all submit
In making all the proposals.

3. It is a matter of conscience
While handling every dealing
To showcase our real prudence
And avoid all the bragging.

4. An experience that is bitter
Should improve your civility
You can't afford to be a quitter
When equipped with agility.

5. For you to be on track
Remove every form of fallacy
Avoid every crack
And create a fruitful legacy...

Chapter 24
Be Close To Your Creator

Being close to our Creator is a fundamental need of every human being. We are all products of a Supreme Creator, and we cannot perform optimally without Him. This calls for our closeness to Him at all times. That is just the healing to our chaotic inner selves, which, in turn, leads to greater productivity and full unlocking of the gifts we are endowed with. If we acknowledge that we were created, then we need to think of our Creator, without whom we shall not be existing. Our closeness to Him is the determining factor for any breakthrough we wish to achieve in life. Without Him, all our supposed gifts and talents are meaningless, as we cannot be in a position to optimise the use of such gifts. There is absolutely nothing we can do on our own. God has the ultimate power. Since all power belongs to Him, our closeness to Him is sacrosanct, so that we can be empowered with the talents we have.

While we will talk about how our closeness to the Creator is tied to the Holy Books, we should note that there are more reasons than being 'religious' to creating a relationship with the all-knowing being. Imagine this: if you have a problem with anything, who best will know how to sort it out other than the person who made it? It is the same with the world. When we go through challenges, evils and others, who do you think can best sort us out? Yes, you are right: Our Creator. Note that depression sets in many times to make us wonder what this world is about. It takes only the grace of the heavens to give us peace. While this might seem outlandish, give it some thought and if you do it, continue. But let us explore more of this closeness to the Creator and why it is important.

Acknowledge God's Presence

It is only a fool that says in his heart: "There is no God" (Psalm 14:1). If you are a reasonable person, you will always acknowledge God's presence in your daily life, and try not to be boastful or proud. The fear of God is the beginning of wisdom. With wisdom, we are highly empowered to make exploits in life.

The reason for us to acknowledge God's presence is that we need to understand that we can do nothing without Him. If we turn our faces to Him, and drop the pride in us, and seek Him, and give Him a chance, He will answer and take care of us and every detail of our lives. In fact, we should recognise the fact that God has never let anyone down. He is the Alpha and Omega.

To acknowledge God's presence, we need to begin each day with a prayer, because He keeps watch over us. Not only should we begin the day with prayer, we should also end the day with prayer. By so doing, we are acknowledging the fact that God is the owner of our lives. Prayer that acknowledges God's ever present power establishes the results of His power. God is there, continuously nurturing and caring for us. Let us always acknowledge His presence in our lives.

Make God Your Friend

If we want to be friends of God, we have to obey Him. The laws have already been outlined in the Holy Books. What we owe Him is our obedience to His Word. God listens, that is why we need to make Him our friend. A true friend always listens to his friend to know what is happening in his life. Our God is a prayer-answering God, so, He is our Best friend.

Making God our friend will avail us the opportunity of understanding that He enjoys spending time with us. He wants us to always come to Him, with whatever burden we may have. God loves us even when we make mistakes, so, why run away from your Creator? Definitely, a good friend is the one that will not despise you. The good train we need to enter is the friendship train of God.

A reliable friend is the one who is always honest. God is honest, and He can never deceive us. We need to enter a good relationship with him, because He will never allow us to perish. Our lives will change for good. When we are discouraged, the only true source of encouragement is God. This is why we need to be friends with Him. He is an awesome God. God is never tired of helping us. He is always available. With Him in our hearts and mind, we make happy and sensible decisions, and surely, accomplish our daily tasks, with an elevated spirit. He makes a way where there seems to be no way. No friend can be more reliable than God. He is the best.

Prayer - The Key To Success

Prayer is the language through which we fellowship with our God. This is a very important ingredient for being close to God. When we pray, we are simply communicating with God. If we do not communicate with Him, how then do we approach Him to take care of our ventures and exploits? Power belongs to

Him and He, alone, can give that power to whom He pleases. If you feel that you are the cause of your greatness or your achievements in life, you are misleading yourself. Without God, nothing is possible; therefore, we owe Him our consistent prayers, either to make our bad conditions to be good, or to make our good conditions to be better. Prayer to our Creator is the way to success.

Peace of mind is produced through prayer. As we pray, we should have faith, not fear, because, God answers the prayers of those who seek Him earnestly. Faith will make us unshakeable in our prayer lives. We should pray without ceasing, as we are always being admonished. There can never be an overdose of prayer. In the family circle, we need to adopt a prayer lifestyle for all the members of the family. In the offices, we need to pray before commencing any activity. In all endeavours, we need to pray first, because, it is the master key to our success in life.

Prayer to God is power-packed. When we pray, believing that we have already received what we are praying for, God answers us. He honours His word. God desires to direct us at every turn, and it is a developed prayer life that will make it easier for Him to guide us. Prayer remains the key word to a successful life.

Constant Touch With The Holy Books

For you to be close to God, you need to be reading your holy books — the Holy Bible, if you are a Christian; or the Glorious Qur'an, if you are a Muslim. It is through these Holy Books that you will get the inspiration about God's worth; it is here you will find information about His word and know the need for you to identify with Him always. The Holy Books awaken and strengthen our faith in God. They surpass all things on this earth.

Through the Holy Book, which is the Word of God, we get hope. We do not always know the path of deepest joy, but all scripture is inspired by God to take us there. Scripture is worth more than all the world can offer. God's Word is your weapon against temptation. We need to deposit it into our hearts, and even memorise it. The Word of God leads us to freedom, because we shall be energised to know the truth, which will set us free. We shall be free from sin, through the Word of God. The truth of God's word works freedom in many ways and brings joy in all of them. God's Word will bring you freedom from hurts, habits, and anxiety. We have been told that, if we continue in His Word, we will transform our thinking to His thinking, and this will bring the truth that will set us free from whatever bondage we are facing.

Our faith is awakened and strengthened through the Word of God. The word that awakens our faith works for our joy. The Word of God creates and sustains our lives. The life we get from bread is fragile and short. The life we get from the Word is firm and lasts forever. The power to overcome sin is through the Word of God. Let us get the word into our hearts. It will lead us to salvation and show us how to live God's way. Reading through God's Word is the same as providing water, soil, and sunlight to a new plant. That is what is needed for God's children to grow. Prosperity and success await us if we are in constant touch with God's Word. When we begin to see as God sees, we will do as God does, and this will lead to prosperity and success.

For us, as human beings, to function normally, our constant touch with the Holy Book will remind us of specific messages that relate to our personal efforts and life challenges. It will teach us new things, guide us when we need direction, and fill us with God's peace. The word of God gives us direction and clarity for our future. When we are confused on the way forward; what to do, and where to go to, we need to read something in the Word that will give the answers to the questions we are asking. Just as our bodies need a balanced diet, our souls require diet of Scripture. Our spirits cannot survive without the Word of God. We nourish our hungry souls when we devote a balanced and generous amount of time to feasting on the truths of Scripture. It revives every famished heart. Just as we do not forget our phones wherever we go to, let us not forget the Holy Books wherever we are.

Honesty, The Best Policy

Closeness to our Creator will be established when we are honest in our thoughts, feelings, and activities, because, God is honest. His 'Yes' is 'Yes', and His 'No' is 'No'. God is pure, and He is purer than any person. So, the purer you are, the more God will touch your heart and fulfil your deepest thoughts. Being honest will definitely draw you closer to your Creator. This attitude will give you mental peace, because you will not live with guilt. This will earn you trust from associates. This characteristic of being trustworthy will distinguish you from others. Lies might ruin your life because of the way they will ruin your relationship with friends, neighbours, family members, colleagues in the office, and so on. There is the tendency for people to move away from you, as you lack the integrity of life.

When we are honest in all aspects of our life, including our marriage, our business, and other relationships, we live the same life wherever we are. This goes on to explain that honesty leads to simplicity, but, dishonesty leads to duplicity. This is because, anytime we are not truthful, we create an alternate reality. This forces us to live a life in both worlds: the true one and the one we have created. With honesty, you will have reliable friends. Since people who are trustworthy and honest influence others positively, with this virtue, you will have the best of friends.

Some people do not know the amount of stress they cause themselves by being dishonest. They will always strive to live on the lies they fabricate. To free yourself from this stressful type of life, you have to be honest, to attract and earn less stress. Of course, when you pretend to be what you are not, you will be stressed up, due to the requirement of not implicating yourself. Honest people relax better, because they are just being themselves and less overwhelmed. Be free from lies.

Be Peaceful

God preaches peace. The two prominent religions in Nigeria, Christianity and Islam, preach peace. For us to be peaceful, we need to resist violence and fight. We have to make our homes, our offices, our educational institutions, our worship areas, our association's gatherings, and so on, peaceful. Being peaceful will enable the glory of God to always shine in us.

In addition to being peaceful, we must always forgive. To err is human, and to forgive, divine. We should have the habit of confessing our sins to our Creator, so that we shall have peace of mind. When our sins are not forgiven, then our prayers to Him are like an abomination unto him, because we are sinners. Let us always have peace in our minds and live in peace with everyone.

Count Your blessings

The habit of counting our blessings will always draw us close to our Creator. It is awesome to note how we are blessed by God. The mere miracle of sleeping and waking up, sound and healthy, is supposed to be highly cherished by us. When we notice the rate of accidents on the way and we are being saved, that calls us to exalt God's name.

We see ourselves passing our exams, while others are failing. We get up each day, and get food on our tables, when some others do not have any loaf of bread to share to family members. We seek the fruit of the womb, and God blesses us with twins, triplets, quadruplets, and so on. We fall sick; visit the hospital and recover, when others are dying. In fact, these tremendous acts of God should attract our closeness to Him, for our gifts to be our full power.

The Holy Books Emphasise This

The Holy Books emphasise that we should be close to our Creator. For instance, in the Holy Bible, the book of Ecclesiastes 12:1 says: "Remember your Creator in the days of your youth, before the days of trouble come and the years approach when you will say I find no pleasure in them." Equally, in the Glorious Qur'an: "Those who have believed and whose hearts find rest in the remembrance of Allah, verily, in the remembrance of Allah do hearts find rest (Q Surah ArRa'd 13:28).

What can we do without our Creator? Of course, nothing! This compels us to note that, in all our endeavours, our closeness to God is of utmost significance; otherwise, we register woeful failures.

It's Really Rewarding
Just as waters of a stream become purer and better as we approach the fountain head, so do our hearts get filled up with blessings from God when we draw closer to Him. Our closeness to our Creator puts us in our proper attitude towards the world. We shall develop positive approaches towards life, because we have been equipped with the power of knowing that our Creator is omniscient, omnipotent, and omnipresent. He has unlimited knowledge and understanding of all things; He has unlimited authority and power; He is present everywhere, at the same time.

In the presence of God, there is fullness of joy. It is little wonder that some people may be physically poor, but, because of their closeness to the Creator, they find joy in their lives. Of course, nothing can buy joy, only God gives it. Nothing on earth can compare with the joy and pleasure of being in God's presence. Once you get the taste, nothing else can ever satisfy you.

God will always fight our battles, and we shall hold our peace. You can never go to the warfare without the sophisticated weapons to defend yourself. Your weapon is your closeness to your Creator. Your attachment to your Creator assures you of His loving kindness and tender mercies, because, He is rich in love and mercy. You will no longer live on the fear of torment by the devil or the world. Being oppressed will be a past story in your life, if you are close to God, because, He executes righteousness and judgement for all that are oppressed. When you are close to Him, He quietens the oppressor, so that he can no longer have power over you.

It pays to be close to God, as we are assured that He will redeem our lives from destruction. This is because He has the power to redeem our lives from the power of the grave and an eternal hell fire. Closeness to our God attracts power to us when we are about to faint on the way. This is because He renews our youth like the eagle. He gives strength to those who have no might. As we get more and more attached to God, He forgives us our iniquities, and this paves way for us to boldly approach the throne of grace in our time of need and ask for help.

Being close to our Creator takes us from a 'mess' to a 'miracle'. This is because He is the one with the ultimate power to change our situations in life. He will redirect our footpaths that will take us to our greater glory. To go away from God will deprive us of being healed of our disturbing diseases and worries. He is the problem solver. Even when we wish to start a project, and we are not equipped on the way forward, He is the one that will show us the way, by either sending someone to assist us, or even opening our own eyes to create new things for ourselves. The experience of our mouths being satisfied with good things is a reward from closeness to God. He becomes our provider if we truly identify with Him. He is the ultimate friend we have to maintain because He alone, is the owner of our lives.

~ To A King Eternal ~

1.   Oh my loving Father
Who will never scatter
All that He has created
To you I remain forever devoted.

2. You take delight in favour
And give me life's true flavour
Your way is ever loving
Keeping me from ever falling.

3. My mouth is full of praises
In life's prevailing phases
His children, He will not deceive
In Him alone, I believe.

4. Recognising I am but sand
Will make me ever stand
To seek your dear righteousness
And bring me close to consciousness.

5. I'll live to ever cherish
How You made me to flourish
In all my circumstances
And the entire chances.

Chapter 25

Potential Unlocked...Destination Reached

66 It is only when you have successfully unlocked your potential that you can be assured that you are at your destination point. You either walk into your story and own it, or you stand outside your story and hustle for your worthiness"— an affirmation from Brene Brown, an American scholar, author, and public speaker. By the time you successfully empower yourself with your gift, you can proudly say you have reached your destination point. This of course, translates to your being successful.

Working Towards Your Goal

Knowing fully that you have the need to reach your destination point requires your articulate way of attaining that goal. Jimmy Dean, a singer, television host, actor, and businessman, sincerely observed thus: "I can't change the direction of the wind, but I can adjust my sails to always reach my destination." This means that you are the one to truly adjust your sails and work towards achieving your goal.

After identifying your talent and realising that it is your gift, you need to move ahead to unfold it through self-confidence and determination, and you will get yourself on top of the ladder. Lack of self-confidence is a trait that is eating deep into the travails of many people who have not been able to make it. The fear of failure is always coming first in such people's minds. Are you a student, a teacher, an administrator, an unemployed, a civil servant, a house wife, a business person? Put a trust in your ability and you will see yourself crossing to the other side of the bridge.

I am encouraged by the quote from Dr Seuss (1904-1991), a writer and cartoonist, which says: "You have brains in your head. You have feet in your shoes. You can steer yourself any direction you choose. You're on your own. And you know what you know. And you are the one who'll decide where to go..."[17]

You are the one who will decide to reach your destination point. Be courageous and daring as, surely, you are trying to venture into risky circumstances, but which will turn out to be for your good, at the end. Working towards your goal will definitely lead you to your desired destination.

The World Is Full Of Opportunities

We are made to understand that the world is full of opportunities. It is best for everyone to find out the most convenient way of tapping them. But, before we go into that, we need to drop our resentments, because, they take too much psychic space for us to be enabled to function properly. This will make our life much lighter. If we develop the ability to think positively, and remind ourselves that we have unique features that can be tapped to reach our destination point, then we are on the right track.

Your feelings are not mere facts, so you have to honour your feelings in order to uphold your calling. You equally need to plan, in order to attain your full potential, because a disorganised person can never get himself right to put things in order. So, things need to be straightened for them to be on course.

Those who have made it in life, have their stories to tell, we must note. Because as Henry Wadsworth Longfellow, an influential American poet, translator, and professor at Harvard University and who was considered the most popular American poet during his lifetime, asserted: "The heights by great men reached and kept were not attained by sudden flight, but they, while their companions slept, were toiling upward in the night." We have to note that the greatness of such men today is their destination point.

The story of Aliko Dangote is one to be reckoned with. Aliko Dangote, Nigerian billionaire and richest black man in the world, (born in 1957) is the founder of Dangote Group. Alhaji Dangote has remained an enterprising man; an attribute noted from his childhood. Despite being born into a wealthy family, he never rested on his oars. He showed interest in business and pursued it faithfully. With his determination, passion and innovation in business across various fields, the entire world keeps hailing him for his ingenuity. He focused his business on the basic necessities of life - food, clothing, transportation and shelter. The Dangote Group activities include cement manufacturing, sugar manufacturing and refining, salt refining, flour & semolina milling, pasta manufacturing, noodles manufacturing, poly products manufacturing, port management & haulage, real estate, and Dangote Foundation. Their goods are practically in almost every home in Nigeria, due to the usefulness of the products. Today, his company is the biggest quoted company in West Africa.

The Dangote Group is equally into corporate social responsibility activities, through the Dangote Foundation. The Foundation provides humanitarian aid to victims of natural disasters, areas of education, health and empowerment. Many indigent students have been privileged to have access to education through the Scholarship opportunities offered by the Dangote Foundation. Dangote's humanitarian gestures know no bounds, as he extends his assistance to other countries outside the shores of Nigeria. His Group intervened during the West African Ebola crisis, the Nigerian flood crisis, the Nepal earthquakes, amongst other numerous interventions.

Regarded as the 'golden child' of Nigerian business circles, Aliko Dangote has offered business opportunities to many people through his various companies. The hue and cry of unemployment would have been too worrisome if not for his patriotism and philanthropy. He is a nonpartisan and detribalised businessman. He is generous to various political parties, religious groups and cultural institutions. Through him, many youths from different ethnic backgrounds have been gainfully employed in the area of product packaging, security, transportation, amongst others. He is a very humble and broad minded man. His wise decision of investing in productive sector demonstrates his level of patriotism. He is a great manager of resources and personnel, and practically demonstrates that one can succeed in business through honesty, determination, and strength of mind. With his level of touching positively on people's lives, he can be considered to have made optimal use of his gift.

Where is your own destination point? Do you even have a vision in life at all? Some people are merely existing, but not really living. Are you focusing on anything at all? What is that potential in you which has not yet been given attention by you? You are the one to unlock that, to pave way for you to reach your destination point in life, as the world is full of opportunities.

Realise Your Personality

Be advised that if you do not realise who you truly are, it will be difficult to honour yourself. Be practical about your personality, so that you can reach your destination point. Changing your life for the better is about picking a destination, and taking one step at a time to get there. Being serious about making improvements is a great start.

Some people do not see anything good each day they wake up, simply because they are '*blinded*' from seeing the sweetness each day offers. Make a point of seeing good in everyday, and you will make your life better. Work with your mind and be friendly with it. You can decide to give yourself a little treat, by visiting an unusual spot, just to give your mind a little relaxation. This goes a long way to cleansing the bitterness that must have accumulated there for long. You will then have a lighter mind to think of useful ventures for yourself.

Always feel relaxed, to pave way for your thoughts and plans to come to fruition. Be at your best always, and value your worth so that you will be in a position to take appropriate decisions for yourself.

A Square Peg In A Round Hole
This is simply putting a person who is unsuited, to the particular position he or she occupies. A peg, literally, is a pin of wood or other material driven or fitted into a platform. The efficacy of a peg is only when it is fixed in a compatible shape, thus, square peg should comfortably match with a square hole, while a round peg will conveniently match with a round hole. A square peg in a round hole is someone who does not fit in.

One of the greatest mistakes some government organisations and employers of labour make is the issue of inappropriate placement and posting of staff who are working for them. This is the main reason for low productivity, and it is detrimental to the growth of the economy. A situation whereby people who can satisfactorily deliver the needed services are relegated to the background, calls for genuine attention, if the government and such employers of labour want the potentials in such individuals to be harnessed.

It is what we feed into the computer that we shall get back. GIGO, which stands for 'Garbage in, Garbage out', is a computer science acronym that implies: 'bad input will result in bad output'. This expression, in the field of Computer Science or Information and Communications Technology, refers to the fact that, computers, since they operate by logical processes, will unquestioningly process unintended, even nonsensical, input data ('garbage in') and produce undesired, often nonsensical, output ('garbage out'). It is impossible to put wrong figures into the machine, and get the right answers. So also, you cannot place the wrong people and get the desired results. A person who is gifted in painting and art work, for instance, needs to be considered for employment in a museum and other related offices. This is to afford him the opportunity to utilise his natural endowment. In the same vein, a gifted person in accounting can comfortably be employed in the banking sector, where he will use his gift.

Placing value on human beings is what will unfold the potentials in such people. People need to be encouraged, in order for the country to get the best. The practice of putting square pegs in round holes should be stopped, so that the desired standards can be attained. One of the effects of such wrong placements is that the work is left to suffer, due to lack of expertise by the ones offered the jobs. Equally, those who are not getting the desired job satisfaction will not be devoted to the job, as they will strongly argue that they cannot fit into such jobs. Of course, you will not blame such people, because, satisfaction comes from the inner mind. You cannot just fake it. It is the fulfilment of the desires, expectations, needs, or demands of the mind. If such claims of non-job satisfaction are considered, and such people are placed appropriately, the sky will be their limit, as job satisfaction is a primary factor for high productivity.

However, as individuals, we should know our strengths and weaknesses. It is only when you know your capability that you can be in a position to fit into a particular job. Your worth is supposed to be of great importance to you, because, that is your power. If you are given an assignment that is above your physical capacity or intellectual power, be humble enough to confess, so that justice can be done to that assignment. If not, you are cheating the government or whoever your employer is. Employers of labour, too, should assign jobs to staff on the basis of merit, rather than on favouritism. The use of technocrats, whether they are related to you or not, is highly encouraged. This is to ensure high level of efficiency. Let us stop deceiving ourselves through wrong approaches. We need to face the reality and speak the truth, because, that is the only thing that can set us free.

Putting a round peg in a round hole is the ultimate. It is a great morale booster. The work will be carried out satisfactorily, because, it is the expert that is handling it. A doctor will conveniently work in the hospital; an engineer will conveniently work in the Works department, and so on and so forth. You cannot fit a square peg in a round hole. The result will just be a misfit. In terms of operational standards of some corporate organisations, the right calibre of people need to be placed there, otherwise, the choice may go contrary to the *modus operandi* of the organisation. Someone who does not fit in to corporate culture, and who is not a team player, is likely unable to attain corporate advancement. The saying: 'Look before you leap', is quite appropriate while we are making decisions, in order to avoid the consequences of putting a square peg in a round hole. This is a clear way to unlocking of one's potential, which in turn, leads one to his destination point.

Change Is Desirable In Life

Change — positive one — is always desirable in our lives. "Your life does not get better by chance, it gets better by change," asserts Jim Rohn, entrepreneur, and motivational speaker. Both educators and parents need to assist the young ones become more purposeful and self-directed in this our rapidly changing world. They need to encourage these young ones to reach their correct destination points. It is easier to catch children, when they are young, for them to be able to develop the right attitudes for success in life.

There is the popular saying: "It isn't what I have, it's what I do with what I have that determines my performance." A child may possess a lot of property without really knowing what to do with any of them. He needs to develop the right frame of mind to handle anything bequeathed to him. The young adults, too, need to decide where they are going to and how to get there. They need to understand that attitude management is a life skill and key to employment success. Without attaining the height you wish for or aim at, you will be having a feeling that you have not fulfilled your purpose in life. Changing your attitude for the better, will definitely help you fulfil your purpose in life.

Remain Focused

Remain focused on your destination point, and have a sense of direction, so that you will get the accurate key for the unlocking of your potential. If you are in the process of transiting towards your full potential, try to prioritise your vision by finding out what makes you happy, and what you can comfortably do. Eliminate the things that do not really have positive impact on you.

The need to commit to a limited number of priorities, instead of concentrating on all, will make you work harder. Of course, you need to create time, by restructuring your laid down schedule, because, life works with us when we learn how to work with it. When you explore possibilities, you are sure to get there. When you do not make attempts, your potential remains locked. Do not be discouraged, because, victory is sure. As you make attempts, and remain focused in attaining your set out goals, you will successfully reach your destination point of success.

Success - A Great Companion And Friend

Success, when achieved, proves to be a great companion and friend. No matter how old you are, what you do, where you live, your ultimate goal in life is to be successful. Being successful is a desirable venture. Success is a good friend. Having a good friend is very important for your happiness. A good friend is someone whose company you enjoy. A successful person will always enjoy success by his side all the time. He enjoys the company, so, to him, it is a great companion. It keeps you on track with people and events.

Your good friend will love you for who you are, so success does that too. It does not look at somebody's face before that person becomes successful. Most of the time, it is merited, either through hard work or God's divine plan. It does not make a choice. You just work for it and earn it. It does not discriminate at all. Anyone who can support you, no matter the situation, is a good friend. When you are successful, the support is already there, it is left to you to look for someone else to support, because you are already successful. Success is a great energy booster, a practical image maker, and a personality motivator. Why would anyone not wish to make it a great companion?

There are friends who are bad, so, those ones cannot be considered to be your real friends at all. A good friend always makes you smile. This is what success can do for you, if it is your friend and companion. Often, we see that successful people are happy people because of the great companionship they find in success. A good friend is kind to you and also respects you, unlike the bad friend, who is always seeking ways to pull you down, seeking ways to destroy you, and seeking ways to stop your progress. Success, on the other hand, gives you progress and kindness. You will always feel high in spirit when success is recorded by you. When you are successful, you will automatically be popular, and this is how your fame crops up. Your new social status becomes a great companion to you.

I totally agree with Michael Bassey Johnson, a poet, playwright, novelist, aphorist, satirist, caricaturist, and a Newspaper columnist, who stated thus: "People will walk in and walk out of your life, but the one whose footstep made a long lasting impression is the one you should never allow to walk out." You should not allow success to slip off your hands, because, it is a great companion. It is the one which has made a long lasting impression in you. It is your great friend.

Since being successful accords you inner harmony, and gives you mental satisfaction, it is a friend indeed. When you are at peace with your mind, what can be more important than that? That is when you will be able to make more exploits. A peaceful state of mind is the best disposition for everyone. You are in company of cool frame of mind. When you are able to unlock the potential in you, you are already at your destination point. Attaining a successful height in life, gives you a feeling of great achievement. Everyone's aim is to be successful, so, you have to aspire to reach that destination point, in order to experience a life of fulfilment.

~ **Your Destination** ~

1. If only there is freedom
To come out from this boredom
It will just take our wisdom
To arrive at our stardom.

2. Through life's unending menace
And jumping out from furnace
And rightly seeking solace
Pushing ourselves to the palace.

3. The driving force to be gallant
Will make you act like giant
And pave way for you to be buoyant
And move on like a merchant.

4. It doesn't take the income
To get the actual outcome
When you make it so gladsome
It turns out to be awesome.

5. Sometimes there comes a delay
But never go for decay
As there will be a display
Which will surely come someday.

Chapter 26
Set To Grab The Keys?

The will to win, the desire to succeed, the urge to reach your full potential — these are keys that will unlock the door of personal excellence, so asserts Confucius (c. 551 to c. 479), a Chinese philosopher, who based his philosophy on the virtues that are required for day to day living. When this door of personal excellence is unlocked, one is set for self-empowerment.

We equally need to be motivated by a statement by the famous American former heavyweight boxing champion, and one of the greatest sporting figures of the 20th century, Muhammad Ali: "Champions are not made in gyms. Champions are made from something they have deep inside them: a desire, a dream, and a vision." This means that the driving force for all achievement comes from within. It is simply a matter of channelling it out. Muhammad Ali (born 1942), was an Olympic gold medallist, and the first boxer to win the world heavyweight championship three times. Definitely, for one to open the door to his house, he needs a key; for one to drive his car, he needs a key. The same applies to life. For one to succeed in life, one needs a set of keys, and the first key is determination and persistence to succeed against all odds. Fortunately, there are various keys that one can use, through determination, to succeed, and fully unlock his potential.

Have A Dream
Dreams are the starting point of all achievement. As our eyes need light to see, so our minds need dreams and ideas to conceive. If, for instance, you are thinking of what will bring you into limelight, you can close your eyes for a moment, try to conceptualise what you feel like doing. As you do so, you need to put your interests into consideration, because, it is what you are happy at doing, what you can freely give out, and what you are capable of doing, that you will think of the most.

You may have a dream of owning a big business centre, a dream of being a renowned footballer, or a dream of being one of the best broadcasters. You will have that concept as your dream, before you can think of realising that dream. Eleanor Roosevelt, America's former First Lady, who we spoke about before, who later served as a United Nations Spokesperson, asserts that: "The future belongs to those who believe in the beauty of their dreams." Have a dream and start working on it.

For instance, if you decide to be a broadcaster, you should start the practice, even while in school, as a member of Press Club, and ensure you involve yourself in the regular broadcast of news in your school. For football, you can start practising with the street boys there. You can play street soccer with children in the neighbourhood and perfect the skills you have.

As you mark your dreams, you need to prioritise your interests. List them out and find out the things that are more important to you, the ones that you can freely offer as services to other people, and the ones that give you joy and happiness. If you enjoy making baskets, for example why not take it up professionally? If you have the ability to make others happy, why not think of being a professional comedian? Your dreams, your inner thoughts, will set you walking. You need to cast off unnecessary things when you are making a choice. Yes, there are activities that are not beneficial and worthwhile to you. It is better to go for the things that will benefit others, so that you can earn credit.

Obey Your Mindset

Napoleon Hill, one of the great writers on success, stated: "Whatever the mind can conceive and believe, the mind can achieve." You need to obey your mind, because, it is the storehouse of incredible potentials. When you make use of an idea that comes into your mind, the mind can easily transform those thoughts into reality, through its magnetic force.

When we have mental determination, our hearts' desires will be achieved more quickly. That is if we add action to our determination. Obeying our hearts' desires and creating that which our hearts compel us to do, will prevent us from having regrets. A certain lady once narrated her devotion to farming to me. She followed a strict routine on a daily basis. The result was that she was able to make a solid future from the occupation. She followed her heart's desire, and she recorded huge success.

Getting In Touch With Your Intuition

This simply means how you can quickly tap into your subconscious mind, which is where you 'archive' all kinds of information that you don't remember on a conscious level. Sometimes, you pick up something subconsciously, but, it registers as a certain 'feeling' that you cannot articulate at that moment, but, it could be valid. Some of the world's greatest scientists, the most logical thinkers of all time, have made their greatest discoveries based on flashes of intuition. A ready example is Newton and the apple that fell on his head.

Sir Isaac Newton was a scientist and great thinker. One day in the season of Autumn, he was lying on the grass, under an apple tree. He was deep in thought, when suddenly, an apple that had grown ripe on its branch, fell to the ground by his side. This provoked a lot of questions from Newton: "What made that apple to fall?" "All heavy things fall to the ground, but why do they?" Millions and millions of people had seen apples fall, but it was left for Sir Isaac Newton to ask why they fall.

He came up with many reasons: "Every object draws every other object towards it" "The more matter an object contains, the harder it draws" "The nearer an object is to another, the harder it draws" "The harder an object draws other objects, the heavier it is said to be" "The earth is many millions of times heavier than an apple, so it draws the apple toward it millions and millions of times harder than the apple can draw the other way" "The earth is millions of times heavier than any object near to or upon its surface, so it draws every such object towards it" "This is why things fall, as we say, towards the earth" "While we know that every object draws every other object, we cannot know why it does so. We can only give a name to the force that causes this" "We call that force *GRAVITATION*" "It is gravitation that causes the apple to fall" "It is gravitation that makes things have weight" "It is gravitation that keeps all things in their proper places." So, this is how he came up with the Law of Universal Gravitation, which states: "Any two bodies in the universe attract each other with a force that is directly proportional to the product of their masses and inversely proportional to the square of the distance between them."

Give yourself breathing space and meditate. When you are confused on making a choice, try to step away from the situation, stand up and go for a long walk. And while you are at it, get some little things you love doing, and start off. Find a quiet space to let your mind wander, and your intuitive voice will have a chance of talking to you. Are you to listen to that little voice in your head? That is the question. Many researchers on intuition have come up with the notion that intuition is far more material than it seems. David Myers, PhD, Hope College, social psychologist, explains that the intuitive right brain is almost always 'reading' your surroundings, even when your conscious left brain is otherwise engaged. The body can register this information while the conscious mind remains blissfully unaware of what is going on.

Equally, a Los Angeles-based intuitive psychiatrist, Judith Orloff, PhD, says: "Your body is a powerful intuitive communicator. Intuition allows you to get the first warning signs when anything is off in your body so that you can address it. If you have a gut feeling about your body – that something is toxic, weak or 'off' – listen to it. Go and get it worked up." In fact, this lady has seen too many people ignore their sense that something was wrong with their bodies, and subsequently, found that small problems later became big ones. We need to listen to the inner mind.

A Burning Desire To Succeed

You need to have a desire for something before you venture into it. Your desires need to be strong enough for you to possess powers to achieve them. It is usually your great convictions that lead you to your great deeds. It is your willpower to reach your success point that will make you pursue your wish vigorously.

In the school set up, for example, a child may have been performing poorly for sometime, but he can suddenly develop a strong willpower to overcome this negative trend. By dissociating himself from all the vices in the school system, and with strong commitment and renewed vigour in his studies, he will definitely succeed. This is not applicable to only the school system, but also the other areas of life endeavours. Unfortunately, some people tag themselves Mr or Mrs 'Failure', after several experienced shortcomings.

Failure, you know, is never one's final point in life. It is rather a motivational force to develop new ways of recording giant strides, with the aim of coming out, successful. You need to rekindle yourself with a new policy of aiming at success at all times. With your mind positively focused, that burning desire in you will earn you success.

Establish A Firm Goal

The first step to realising your dreams is to establish a firm goal around which to organise your thoughts and plan a path of vision. Your goal is your dream, but with a deadline. A lot of people do not spend enough time to think about what they want from life, and consequently, have not set themselves formal goals. Setting goals gives you a sense of direction. You can know where to concentrate your efforts on by the time you know what you want to achieve. This will enable you frustrate any type of distraction that might crop up.

You need to set goals that motivate you. This means making sure they are important to you, and that there is value in achieving them. Motivation is the key to achieving goals. Your priority list will assist you in setting your goal. You are the one who wish to achieve something, so, your goal achievement requires commitment. If you do not have a positive approach to the realisation of your goal, you will end up being disappointed and frustrated with yourself. It is even necessary to write down why that desire is valuable and important to you.

Your goal will be powerful if it is specific, measurable, attainable, relevant, and bound by time. Goal setting not only allows you to take control of your life's direction, it also provides you a benchmark for determining whether you are actually succeeding or not. Try to stick to your goals. Build in reminders so that you will always be kept on track. From time to time, you need to review your goals, to ascertain if you are still on track. The relevance, value, and necessity, should remain high. A firm goal, definitely, leads to eventual realisation of your life desires.

Paddle Your Own Canoe

You should explore and discover new things and consequently, work on them. Some people are easily discouraged and continue to lean on other people's successes while they can easily stand on their own and make a mark. If you succeed in making a breakthrough, it is your achievement. St. Augustine of Hippo, one of the greatest theologians of Western Christianity, in this light stated: "Go forth on your own path, as it exists only through your walking." Fear should be completely cast away from you, so that you can be daring to make new discoveries. Merely waiting for opportunities to occur before you make moves means that you are not ready to dream and make what seems impossible to be possible.

Set Your Imagination Free – Be Creative

You can set your imagination free by being creative. This is the willingness to stop, and look at things that no one else has bothered to look at. This process of focusing on things that are normally taken for granted is a powerful source of creativity, according to Edward de Bono, widely regarded as one of the foremost experts in the field of creativity and lateral thinking.

You may not be fully skilled in a particular profession but you can make great achievements through creative thinking. Creativity involves stepping into the unusual. You are the one to initiate the action and the skills to use. Most creative ideas will seem silly at first, but people need to get used to creativity. It will eventually turn to be something meaningful. Some children can simply pick up a piece of paper and use that to create a lot of funny things like a kite, a boat, a table, a chair, and so on. Since there are no new ideas really, you can borrow the old ideas and make combinations. This is creativity. It is your own original perception — a new idea emerges. While undergoing this, you have to cast away doubts and fears. Challenge yourself to success.

You may face criticism while trying to be creative but be brave. Creativity demands much courage and self-confidence, so that you will remain focused on what you want to achieve. Do not be afraid to be wrong in your creativity bid. You can never get it right if you do not make mistakes. You need to persevere to the end of realisation of your dear imagination. Rather than ask 'Why?', ask 'Why not?' It will push you into doing something extraordinary. There is no reason for doing nothing, and there is every reason for doing something. Whatever you do counts, just because you are actually doing it.

Abraham Maslow (1908 - 1970) was an American psychologist, best known for creating Maslow's hierarchy of needs, a theory of psychological health predicated on fulfilling innate human needs in priority, culminating in self-actualisation. On the value of thinking and being imaginative, he famously stated: "Every great advance in science has issued from a new audacity of imagination."

When you start being creative, you will set your imagination free. What are you waiting for?

Draw A Schedule

You are not expected to get stuck up in your work. You should make a timetable in such a way that there is time for everything, so that you can have room for better productivity. For you to get better productivity, you have to take breaks, eat lunch away from your work area, focus on tasks, drink plenty of water, get plenty of rest, read often, write often, plan ahead, keep record. Dabbling into any activity at any time, without a schedule, will make you look disorganised, and subsequently, cause low production on your part. Make yourself better organised.

Do Not Procrastinate

The time to act is now. When you are in the habit of putting off or delaying, especially something requiring immediate attention, you are procrastinating. Jim Rohn, a foremost American business philosopher, a personal development legend, advised thus: "It doesn't matter which side of the fence you get off sometimes. What matters most is getting off. You cannot make progress without making decisions."

Procrastination prevents people from reaching their goals and objectives. Most of the time, it is due to laziness that people keep on postponing what they are supposed to do. This, in turn, results to very low turnout in productivity. Whatever it is in business or in academics, this practice is very bad. Any businessman or Executive who keeps on postponing an important management meeting on how to improve the company or the office, is indirectly pulling that place down. In the same vein, any student who keeps on postponing his study schedule is only planning to fail. That is just that.

This practice is neither acceptable in one's personal life nor in one's occupation. This is because procrastination increases the chances of losing many opportunities such as rewards, promotions, or special recognitions in one's employment. Due to procrastination, people miss deadlines, miss their flights, miss job opportunities, miss admission into institutions of their desire, and so on. Really, this can lead to stress, because, a lot of things are kept and left undone. This is an unhealthy situation, and can never allow one to unlock his potential fully.

Keep Your Body Fit

Exercises will give you a surge of energy each day, and help your brain make creative connections. Exercise is one of the greatest keys of unlocking one's potential. If you want to feel better, have more energy and perhaps, live longer, you need to be involved in physical exercises, to enable your blood flow freely. Exercise improves your mood. Your emotion can be positively boosted when you exercise yourself.

Your health conditions get better when you get involved in exercises, because, they combat the diseases in your body. Regular exercises can help you prevent health problems like stroke, metabolic syndrome, high blood pressure, heart attack, depression, and so on. Exercise controls weight, and helps prevent weight gain. As you engage in physical exercises, you burn calories. The more intense the activity, the more calories you burn. This makes you feel lighter and energetic to carry on the task you wish to accomplish. Boosting of energy is attained through regular exercise. It can improve your muscle strength and boost your endurance.

Of equal note is that exercise promotes sleep. Some people struggle to sleep at the end of the day's work. This is quite unhealthy, because the brain needs to relax well before the next day's activities take off. However, regular exercise will put you in the mood of proper sleeping at bedtime. The physical exercise performed will allow you to have a very deep and sound sleep. After the sound sleep, one wakes up the following day, hale and hearty.

Exercise is fun. It gives one the chance to feel free and mix with others in activities like dancing, athletics, cycling, tennis, and volleyball. That is the time to shout with joy. That is the time to laugh freely. One imagines the quantity of joy football fans and footballers, for example, receive each time they are engaged in this type of exercise in the field. That is the time both old and young, think alike, and rejoice exceedingly. When your body is positively stimulated through exercises, you can be sure of great performance in any venture you want to undertake. Just take some time off to exercise, and 'smell the roses'.

Let Go Of The Past

The past cannot be changed; the future is still in our hands. If you focus on the present, you will have less time to think of the past. Since you cannot undo the past, make today the best day of your life. Stephen Covey, an American educator and keynote speaker, stated: "I can change. I can live out my imagination instead of my memory. I can tie myself to my limitless potential instead of my limiting past." This is for those who want to forge ahead and forget the past hurts.

As you move on in life, your goals and needs will definitely change. What was right for you before may not necessarily be right for you now. If all you do is attempt to relive something that has already happened, you are not making any progress. You need to let go of things that are already behind you, so that you will be able to fill the space with something fresh.

You have to be thankful for all the experiences that made you laugh, cry, and even helped you learn and grow. You also have to be thankful for the possibilities that lie ahead. Focus only on what can be changed. Take full control of your life. No one else is responsible for you. If you want to change, if you want to let go and move on with your life, you are the only one who can make it happen.

Life moves in only one direction – forward. We move into the future, and never into the past. This is your chance to let go of the old and make way for the new. Your destiny awaits your decision. Your motto should be: 'Forward, ever; backward, never'. Always be ready to learn something new and not to stick to the past knowledge. Forget the past miserable experiences. Do not lean on your past mistakes. Greater and better things are happening each new day.

Develop Positive Attitude

We need to understand that a positive attitude reduces negative emotions; it helps you find more fulfilment and enjoyment in life, and will enable you recover from negative experiences more quickly. "It isn't what you have or who you are or where you are or what you are doing that makes you happy or unhappy, it is what you think about it," — so asserts Dale Carnegie, an American writer and lecturer, and the developer of famous courses in self-improvement, salesmanship, corporate training, public speaking, and interpersonal skills. Carnegie is the author of *How To Win Friends and Influence People* (1936), a massive bestseller that remains popular today, and *How To Stop Worrying And Start Living* (1948), and several other books. One of the core ideas in his books is that it is possible to change other people's behaviour, by changing one's behaviour toward them.

With positive attitude to life, you will develop great and harmonious relationships. People will love your lifestyle and will get easily attracted to you. As a matter of fact, positive mind attracts positive events. We need to develop positive attitude, to improve our attention, creativity, and ability to learn; it also improves our ability to cope with difficult situations. Due to the fact that it reduces stress, it improves your overall well-being. You will have vibrant health with a positive attitude. Kind thoughts take care of your health and you cannot have stress issues. The main cause of stress is worry and negative thoughts. Positive people overcome stress more easily.

It is worthy to state that if you have positive attitude or thinking, all your problems and challenges will be turned into opportunities to make new exploits, and consequently, this will earn you abundance of good things in your life, just as beauty will start shining from within. Stay positive in your thoughts always, for you to be in a position to grab the keys of success.

~ **Right In My Arms** ~

1. As I'm fully activated
I'm equally motivated
Holding the keys for champions
Which are serving as my companions

2. The ladder of eminence
Requires my excellence
I'm adjusting my mindset
To grab that precious asset

3. Idle minds I will astonish
Good things I will accomplish
With my canoe I will paddle
Moving from my own cradle.

4. What else than my willingness
To move on without selfishness
And nobody to betray,
But my image to portray.

5. A life devoid of displeasure
Pursued with great endeavour
Using all the good discretion
Will reach a glorious perfection.

CONCLUSION

Once you are able to recognise that you have a gift, then, you are on the path of greatness. It is left to you to develop that gift, because, that is your power! Your neighbour out there may not be so lucky to possess what you have, so, why waste your own?[18]

As a human being created by the all-knowing Creator of the universe, you need to acknowledge that you have been endowed with a special gift. This gift is your talent, so to say and you need to use it to unlock the potential in you, for the greatness in life you so much desire. Be conscious of dangerous games people play, so that you will not be a victim of such. In your bid to climb the ladder of life and success, do not forget your positive impact on others will make much difference. Through creative thinking, you will be able to jump the difficult hurdles that trail everyone on the path to success.

Note too that as you embark on this journey, you are bound to make mistakes. But do not live in the past. Focus on the future, by building on your mistakes. Learn from failure and build on it to be better. Since you desire success, you need to identify fully with it. It is important to share also because you don't know who will help you find a solution to certain problems you might have or who your story might help. So, endeavour to share your experience with others, so that learning can take place: either yours, theirs or both parties'.

The need to always be yourself will always make you to be up and out. As you make humility your watchword, you will find out that you can easily adapt to strange environments and always move with trends. Equally, as you become friendlier, people will cherish you and refrain from hurting you. You also have to take charge, be firm and resolute in all your ways. This will shield you from intimidation, as you will always stand firm and be yourself. As you strive to be a role model, you will find out that you will be making judicious use of your time, being always conscious of time. This evidently makes time your good friend, as you will always be guided by it. While determining your goal in life, you will see yourself initiating a selling point that will catapult you to your *El Dorado*.

Of course, as you get committed to finding a firm ground, no form of idleness will – or should - locate you. With the spirit of optimism fired by enthusiasm, you will find out that all your disappointments will turn into blessing for you. With all these traits, you will be in a position to show the light to others, and, equally, be on guard, to maintain the discipline that has taken you to that height. Realising that it is through the divine inspiration and empowerment from God that you can scale through in life, you will be automatically drawn close to Him. Fully embracing God will equip you with all the necessary keys that will unlock your potential, thereby leading you to your destination point, which is success.

Come on, showcase your gift. Just as your vote during elections is your right and power, so also, your gift is your power. You are the one to bring it into limelight. A golden fish has no hiding place; so, do not make any attempts to hoard that gift. Use it, and make it your power. Always be motivated and bask in the knowledge as you work to make it count that, *your gift is your power!*

~ NOTES ~

CHAPTER 2

1. (Page 12) Retired Super Eagles star regarded as one of the most decorated African footballers. Kanu won several awards for different football clubs across different European leagues. He was part of the 1996 Dream Team that won the gold medal in football at the Atlantic 96 Olympics. Kanu also captained the Nigerian team to some world cups and African Cup of Nations tournaments before eventually retiring.

2. (Page 12) Austin 'Jay Jay' Okocha is an ex-Super Eagles star who captained the Nigerian national team to different world cup tournaments. He was part of the 1996 Dream Team that won the gold medal in football at the Atlantic 96 Olympics. He plied his trade across different clubs in Europe including Bolton Wanderers and PSG. He is regarded as one of Nigeria's finest dribblers and was a master dazzler with his feet world over during his playing days.

3. (Page 13) Only recently, Chimamanda was awarded the 'Bailey of the Baileys'. She won the Orange Prize for Fiction (as the Baileys was called then) in 2007. Her award of Bailey of the Baileys shows that her book, Half of a Yellow Sun was selected as the best Bailey award recipient in the history of the awards.

CHAPTER 3

4. (Page 19) Sir Winston Churchill (1875-1965) is regarded as one of Britain's finest Prime Ministers and the greatest Prime Minister of the 20th Century. He was Prime Minister in World War II and was instrumental in the victory that led to the ultimate defeat of Hitler and Germany. In many quarters, Churchill is said to have been bigger than Britain itself. He was awarded the Nobel prize for Literature in 1953 for his historical and biographical work and his oratory.

CHAPTER 5

5. (Page 35) From Anne Frank – Diary of a Young Girl. United States: Doubleday & Company, 1952.

6. (Page 37) Like the West African School Certificate Examination (WASCE) by the West African Examination Council (WAEC) and Senior School Certificate Examination (SSCE) by the National Examination

Council (NECO) for those in Nigeria.

CHAPTER 6

7. (Page 44) Mark Twain, American author of the famous Huckleberry Finn and Tom Sawyer series, is regarded as one of the most prominent American authors of the 19th century. His works marked a departure from the formal writing that characterised American literature and formed the basis for a more nationalist writing.

CHAPTER 7

8. (Page 50) Albert Einstein (1879-1955) was not generally thought of in high esteem by his tutors. He spent a lot of time studying on his own. He contributed greatly to social and political causes. He also wrote great books including Why War? (co-written with the equally famous Sigmund Freud, and published in 1933). Einstein was once offered the position of President of Israel, a position he famously rejected.

CHAPTER 9

9. (Page 65) Eleanor Roosevelt was the wife of Franklin D. Roosevelt (1882-1945), the 32nd and longest serving President of the United States of America (1933-1945). Eleanor had an active public career before and during her marriage and continued to maintain a high profile even after her husband's death. She was a lifelong champion of poor and marginalised people and is also known to have been the original person to make the famous comment: 'No one can make you feel inferior without your consent.'

10. (Page 65) V' stands for Vincent, his name.

11. (Page 68) Charlotte Brontë is one of the famous Brontë sisters (including Emily and Anne) whose works have come to be regarded as some of the most revered classics in English literature.

CHAPTER 10

12. (Page 73) Theodor Seuss Geisel (1904-1991), more known with is pen name 'Dr. Seuss', was an American author and artist, who wrote popular children's books. He sold millions of books that have continued to entertain generations of children while helping them to read.

CHAPTER 12

13. (Page 85) For more information on this, you can easily refer to Turner T. Isoun and Miriam J. Isoun's *Why Run Before Learning to Walk: Reflections on High Technology as a Strategic Tool for Development in Nigeria* (Ibadan: BookBuilders, 2013).

CHAPTER 14

14. (Page 100) Chinedu Ikedieze and Osita Iheme (a.k.a 'Aki' and 'Pawpaw' respectively) have carved a niche for themselves in the Nollywood despite their being considered dwarfs due to their smallish statures. They have acted over a hundred movies and are a household name in Nigeria and the world.

CHAPTER 16

15. (Page 110) From Ernest Hemingway's *The Old Man and the Sea* (New York: Simon &Schuster, 1952).

16. (Page 111) Jesse Jackson campaigned as a candidate for the Democratic party's nomination to be President of the United States of America in 1984 and 1988.

CHAPTER 25

17. (Page 181) From the children's book, *Oh! The Places You'll Go!*

CONCLUSION

18. (Page 199) Of significant interest to me is the write-up by Gene N. Landrum, Ph.D, a lecturer and the creator of the Chuck E. Cheese concept of family entertainment, which stated thus: "The 'greats' have eight key behavioural traits critical to their success. Eight keys to Greatness selects six diverse disciplines and those who achieved within them - the Arts (Agatha Christie and Ernest Hemingway); Business (Bill Gates and Helena Rubinstein); Humanities (Mother Theresa and Martin Luther King Jr.); Politics (Catherine the Great and Mao Tse-tung); Science (Albert Einstein and Marie Curie); and Sports (Michael Jordan and Babe Didrickson Zaharias) - to show that charisma, competitiveness, confidence, drive, intuition, rebellion, risk-taking, and tenacity, led these celebrities to the top."

~About The Author~

Helen Uche Ibezim was born at Enugu into the family of late Mr. Vincent Okoli Egbo (from Ohukabia village of Nawfijah town in Orumba South LGA of Anambra state) on 31st July 1964. She graduated from the University of Nigeria, Nsukka with Second Class Honours (Upper Division) in French. She obtained her Post Graduate Diploma in Education from same University; Diploma in Computer Studies & Information Technology; Certificate in Creativity (New York City, USA); West African School Certificate (WASC); General Certificate in Education (GCE); Diplôme de Langues, Littérature et Civilisation Françaises from Université de Grenoble III, France. She is an old student of Queen's School, Enugu.

She has served as a classroom teacher, a Head of Department in a secondary school system, a Dean of Studies, a Senior Mistress (Academics), a Vice Principal (Administration), a School Principal in FCT, and, an Inspector of Education. She is a Deputy Director at FCT Universal Basic Education Board, Abuja.

She has been recognised in a number of ways, such as: Award of *'Woman of Vision'*, Award of *'Excellence'*, Award of *'Mother of Faith'*, Investiture as *'Lady of the Knight of St.Christopher'*, Investiture as a Matron of the Scouts Association of Nigeria, Karu District, FCT, Abuja. Prior to the publication of this book, Helen Uche Ibezim had written a number of articles in magazines & journals; served as Resource Person in many educational functions; and served as Editor in *'RSL'* and *'The Light'* magazines.

Uche has international experiences from France, South Africa, United Arab Emirates, Italy, United States of America, West Germany, Egypt, République du Bénin, Israel, United Kingdom, and Switzerland. She is happily married to Commander Angus Obum Ibezim (from Ovollo village, now Anioma, in Mbaukwu town of Awka South LGA of Anambra state), a staff of the Federal Road Safety Corps, Nigeria. They are blessed with children.

www.ingramcontent.com/pod-product-compliance
Lightning Source LLC
Chambersburg PA
CBHW030825090426
42737CB00009B/871